A Gaffer's
PERSPECTIVE

on

INDEPENDENT
FILMMAKING

A Gaffer's
PERSPECTIVE

on

INDEPENDENT FILMMAKING

PRACTICES, TECHNIQUES
and
TRICKS of TRADE REVEALED

RICK M. LORD

Universal-Publishers
Boca Raton

A Gaffer's Perspective on Independent Filmmaking:
Practices, Techniques, and Tricks of the Trade Revealed

Universal-Publishers
Boca Raton, Florida • USA
2011

ISBN-10: 1-61233-059-2
ISBN-13: 978-1-61233-059-4

www.universal-publishers.com

Cover photo © Kaarsten | Dreamstime.com

Cover design by Shereen Siddiqui

Layout by delaney-designs.com

Library of Congress Cataloging-in-Publication Data

Lord, Rick M., 1954-
   A gaffer's perspective on independent filmmaking : practices, techniques, and tricks of the trade revealed / Rick M. Lord.
       p. cm.
   ISBN-13: 978-1-61233-059-4 (pbk. : alk. paper)
   ISBN-10: 1-61233-059-2 (pbk. : alk. paper)
   1. Independent films--Production and direction. 2. Cinematography. I. Title.
   PN1995.9.P7L67 2011
   791.4302'32--dc23
                                                    2011035385

Table of Contents

PART TWO

Chapter Twelve

Chapter Thirteen

Introduction

The fact that you're reading this book is testament that you can be reasonably sure the fascination and lure of filmmaking comes from deep within. To command your very own movie production is a drive that overwhelms you like a bad cold, but where does one begin?

If ever there was an industry that travels down the "Catch-22 highway," it's the motion picture industry. Unless you have moviemaking experience in your past, how will you ever have moviemaking experience in your future? How does one get experience? Allow me to introduce you to the ways of the no/low budget, independent film.

Lights, camera, action, and your dreams are finally a reality! The script has been re-written so many times the letters on the keyboard of your laptop are worn to the point of non-recognition. All of the pre-production details have been accomplished with every "i" dotted and every "t" crossed and now there's only one thing left to do. Put it on film, digitally speaking that is...

It's 4:00 AM and the call sheet reads "Day One" of twenty-three. You're running on pure adrenaline due to the fact that you haven't had but fifteen minutes of sleep within the past twenty-four hours. The art department is still meticulously dressing the set and tweaking props and furnishings. The actors are sitting in make-up while you, along with the DP, gaffer and key grip, are choreographing camera positions and making final lighting tweaks.

A shout goes out to one of the PAs to bring you a double shot "venti latte" and as you take your first sip of the life-enlightening elixir, the talent, at last, walks onto set. After a few exchanges of light dialogue, you place the actors on their marks and begin blocking rehearsal. Make-up also steps in for final touches, and then the call from the first AD to roll camera is heard over the entire set. Camera speed, sound speed, and now the time has come to bark your first command of the production, "Action!" You're on your way to making your first independent film.

Producing an independent film can be a lot of fun. There's no sweeter glory than experiencing days and days of movie making at its best. There's no reason the experience of making an independent film has to turn into a stringing together of miserable days of conflict and countless technical snafus.

In conscious defense, no one exits the womb with a director's viewfinder and a light meter in hand. Everyone in this industry starts from somewhere and has to go through the pains and angst of his or her very first production. For whatever reason, there's that deep down propensity to believe the very first film you produce is going to be "The One," the one that has you standing at the podium thanking all the little people who made it possible. Yes, there are those few individuals that who shoot out of the gate with a piece of work that grabs the masses, but for most, it's just a "pie in the sky" daydream. After working on my fair share of independent films as a gaffer, I've seen it all -- some good, and others, not so much. Poor planning, bad scripts, and lack of experience have doomed many a production. I cannot tell you how many filmmakers quit after their first film

After the experience of having a first production go so horribly awry, they'd rather find themselves driving dump truck in Grafton, North Dakota, never to return to filmmaking ever again. This does not need to be the case. Independent filmmaking can, for the most part, be fun and rewarding. That is, of course, if serious attention to thorough preparation is made.

I've had some of the greatest experiences of my life as a gaffer. It is my opinion that this position has the greatest viewpoint of the overall filmmaking process. The opportunity to see first hand what makes for a great production is, itself, an awesome gift. To invent, create and experience the filmmaking process satisfies not only the artistic side of the brain, but the technological side as well. Notwithstanding, it's the experiences I have had over the years that have exposed the truly gifted as well as the truly troubled.

Over many decades, the business of filmmaking has been refined to an absolutely scientific process. In other words, there is a proper way in which to carry out all necessary tasks to accomplish such an endeavor. Almost anyone these days can pick up a camera and call him or herself a filmmaker. However, this is a dog eat dog business and it's only those who have learned to apply the fundamental proven-to-work-processes to the art and business of film making, who stand a chance in experiencing success.

As far as film schools go, I couldn't tell you for sure whether or not it is money well spent. I do know there have been plenty of interns who have crossed my path and have walked away discouraged. Their comments are many times the same. "I didn't learn any of this in film school." There's obviously a difference between book smarts and street smarts. In other words, what is learned in the classroom and what is learned on the set are often two different worlds.

Does a degree in filmmaking help? I'm sure it does, but so does knowing how to head wrap a BJ. I've often suggested to those that wish to enter into the movie making business, try it first and see if you really like it. Where would you like to see yourself five or ten years down the road? Getting hired as an intern Production Assistant is as easy as feeding a cupcake to a monkey, and as an intern one can observe and gravitate towards the positions that are of greatest interest and plan, from there, a career choice. If then your chosen position requires getting a degree in filmmaking, great. Be forewarned, a degree in this industry is many times not worth the paper it's printed on. Sad but true, success many times comes down to the "it" factor. You either have "it" or you don't.

This book is dedicated to those no/low budget independent filmmaker wannabe types, who wish to take on Hollywood with their own artistic vision. That being said, there are still those tried and true practices that have been developed over the years that are proven to work.

There's only one way to effectively convey the processes that do work... Share with you the bad processes that don't work. Many of the examples I refer to are from some productions that have tried the unconventional approach and failed. I have also created scene and story scenarios that, by design, are to lead and teach. They are examples only, such as the bistro scene, which is referred to throughout the book.

This manuscript is separated into two parts. The first part is devoted to the inner political processes that deem sane movie making practices. It is these practices that also teach what to look for in key personnel that will ensure a greater chance of achievement. In addition, it serves as an introduction to the psychological aspects of filmmaking all must be aware of. Part two is devoted to the technical aspects of the motion picture making processes. By design, part two is to teach the photographic sciences and techniques that are inherent to the process of filmmaking. These sciences, understood and applied, will without a doubt, indemnify the creative.

PART ONE

Chapter One

REALITY CHECK

As mentioned in the foreword, there is only one way to approach filmmaking. Do as those who have marched on before have done or, at the very least, come close to how the big guys make movies. The processes of filmmaking have been around for decades. Re-inventing the wheel or trying to circumnavigate tried and true methods and procedures will only result in one painful frame of film after another. That said, it is also important to understand that the no/low budget, independent film making process does come with its own inherent idiosyncrasies. For instance, compared to the filmmaking procedures that are associated with the huge union-sanctioned Hollywood mega-flicks, the no/low budget rules of engagement are often accomplished by more of a "seat-of-the-pants" approach, which means fewer individuals wearing more hats. In other words, sharing duties with other departments is many times common practice. Money, or the lack thereof, is the reason for this dichotomy. Not only does money determine the degree of overall production value, it determines how many bodies will be on set to do the work at any given time. Money also determines the level of experience that will be associated with any given production. Is it Cousin Eddie on camera, brother Delbert on sound, and Aunt May expressing her creative talents as set decorator? It takes more than a desire to make a movie. Besides money, it takes tons of logistical planning and more than just a few trained individuals to have even the smallest of chance of being successful.

Big Budget versus No/Low Budget

The independent film market has come a long way over the past few years; it's no longer dismissed as some high school wannabe film project that spits out silver-screen dribble. Independent films of today have become serious contenders, even in Hollywood terms. "Independent" simply refers to a film's non-connection to the typical Hollywood studio-backed project. Nonetheless, the independent film market has become a visual art, not to be taken lightly.

There are more than just a few differences between inner-departmental responsibilities when comparing the major motion picture to the independent no/low budget film. In the major leagues, department classifications dictate what equipment you are free to work with and what equipment you are not free to work with. If, for example, a person in the grip department begins messing around with electrical department things, it's back to the French-fry machine. In contrast, this is many times the opposite when working on an independent no/low budget film. Only on a no/low budget independent film can a PA (Production Assistant) be promoted to focus puller for an afternoon, or the craft service lady fall from a two-story building for the big stunt scene. As crazy as this may sound, it's these departmental line-crossing practices that make the no/low budget film production process so much more fun and interesting to work on. Now take the DP (Director of Photography) and gaffer positions. They also cross each other's department lines much of the time in the no/low budget world. It is often their knowledge and expertise that together paints the scenes with light, makes lens choices, and creates that ever sought after million-dollar camera move. Taking it one step further, the new DP is many times the owner of the camera. This would then suggest he or she is, no doubt, the writer, director, gaffer, key-grip and craft service person.

For the major big dollar productions, it's the Director of Photography who paints the scene with light. It is he or she who chooses the desired lenses, camera positions, framing, and movement that best tells the visual part of the story for the director. The DP is the one who brings to the project his or her creative interpretation, artistic style and vision. Many times DPs are chosen because of their expressive signature style of cinematography.

So what about the gaffer and the rest of the bunch when it comes to the big budget filmmaking process? The gaffer is the chief electrician, the person who is the head lighting technician. Does the gaffer choose and place lights? To some extent the answer is yes, but usually by the request and direction of the DP. The lights are labored into position by the gaffer's crew of electricians, and the best boy electric is responsible for the proper distribution of electrical power to all lighting instruments. Last but not least, the key grip and his or her department set the stands, flags and scrims that control and shape said light. In other words, it's the big picture productions that can afford to hire experienced key personnel and their crew to handle each of the many departmental requirements.

This brings us to a sad but very true fact. Those who begin their careers in the no/low budget indie biz often fail to learn the correct processes of making movies, unless they have ventured into the larger union productions for a time, or at the very least, read a few books and watched a few videos on the subject. The lack of money to do things the way the big boys do things is certainly challenge number one. This would suggest that having enough money to hire a few key people who know what the heck they're doing will help close the gap between big budget filmmaking processes and the cousin Eddie backyard approach.

As the gaffer on a recent production, I had the same challenges that face most gaffers on no/low budget films, only on a much greater scale.

A director friend of mine, who was also the writer of the screenplay, had a novel idea. He wanted to see if he could film an entire movie without any money to invest into the project. Obviously there would be some money for the absolute must haves, such as food and a few grip and electric rental items along with a Honey Bucket (porta-potty) or two, but no real big money, the kind of money one would expect to spend on a movie production. He had actually written a great script and it was almost a shame to waste it on an experiment such as this. His thought was if the experiment indeed worked as planned, he would have a no/low budget independent film with a huge profit potential; however, this concept would become a very risky undertaking.

Under the Walnut Tree… No Plan for Disaster

Welcome to "Under the Walnut Tree." While the title has been changed to protect the innocent, this particular production has many similarities with other failed movie making endeavors. The one saving grace for this production was the director, who brought to the table many exceptional attributes not often realized with new directors. It was those keen attributes that kept the project from folding up like a cheap suit on Day One. Even though the director was young and had limited experience, his dedication to perfection and his willingness to accept counsel from those with greater knowledge made it possible for such a production to take place.

The DP was also young and new to the industry. His training was primarily of a video background. Just like many before him, he sported his lighting package of choice, his trusty Lowell Kit. Understanding everyone must start somewhere, he was indeed the typical wedding photographer turned DP we've all come accustomed to working with in no/low budget filmmaking. It was clear right from the start that the entire production was going to need strong support and knowledgeable counsel to ensure the film making process would indeed be successful. Even though it was difficult, it was up to us with more experience to help by mentoring with quiet, unassuming authority.

As I've alluded to, making a success of any film project without sufficient funds is beyond ludicrous, to say the least; however, add to that a lack of proper planning, and watch movie making go to a whole new level of crazy.

What began on August 9th as an experiment would turn into a complete disaster by August 10th. There was no real pre-production and the schedule had fallen apart almost immediately. No viable reality check as to how to overcome some pretty big hurdles meant there was no guarantee that a successful production could be made. With no solid logistical plan and many key positions dismissed as too costly, the production was crippled from Day One. An inexperienced producer who was interested in title only, also suggested failure. Along with no UPM (Unit Production Manager) and no first AD (First Assistant Director), the production was pretty close to being doomed right from the start.

Unfortunately many no/low budget independent film projects set out on a path of self-destruct because of this very same misguided approach.

There must be a viable concrete plan of attack when setting out to accomplish the task of producing any film, otherwise one might as well head off into the sunset with camera in hand and hope something interesting jumps in front of the lens.

The harsh reality of it all, despite the term of "no/low budget", is that it's going to cost money. The very moment a script is in-hand, the pre-production phase should be well under way. Questions concerning plausibility, logistics and schedules come into play immediately unless only seen through a haze of bong smoke. It is during the pre-production phase that the reality check button is pushed; thus, the first big question arises. Is the story even feasible?

Having no plan is a plan to fail.

Chapter Two

THE PRE-PRODUCTION FUNCTION

Interesting fact: Did you know that the new car you've had your eye on first hit the drawing board some three to five years ago? I find it truly astounding that thousands of people had the foresight so many years ago to design and build a viable, desirable product scheduled for today's driver. So the question arises, why should the making of any motion picture be anything less? A goal to create that viable, desirable product should be at the forefront of every filmmaker's mind as well. How is this accomplished? The answer is pre-production.

Going back to "Under the Walnut Tree," the pre-production phase of this film was all but nonexistent. Their initial attempt at assembling a schedule, which was ten days at ten pages per day, was the first big red flag that indicated things were not going to go well. Ever since principal photography began, the project failed to make its pages on any given day. Between screaming matches, and cast and crew threatening to quit, this production was a train wreck before ever leaving the station. There were constant wardrobe, prop and continuity snafus that plagued almost every scene. There were locations that were more difficult to shoot on than if we'd chosen planet Mars. The disgruntled production finally came to a bitter wrap a whopping forty-eight days later. Why all of the turmoil? No pre-production, no plan of attack.

The process of pre-production, if executed properly, will guarantee a successful project from the first day to the very last day. Pre-production begins with the script. From the first day a script is written, purchased or stolen, pre-production is, or should be, running at full throttle. Does this guarantee a money making film? No, but it does suggest there'll be fewer dead bodies and at the very least, a complete film.

The Script

Whether a script is purchased from a professional writer or personally written, the first question to be answered is this: is the story realistic to film with the budget given? If the story opens with the two lead characters aboard the space shuttle Endeavor during re-entry, and the budget is less than the value of a '79 Ford Fairmont, you're likely to be greatly disappointed. Even with all of your close NASA connections, that scene is probably going to be unrealistic to produce. The ultimate goal is to have a workable script to start with, something you can actually accomplish with the meager budget at hand.

Early in my career I was talking with a director friend of mine when I made the comment, "I'd like to write and film a Western someday. Cowboys, Western towns, horses, buckboards and stagecoaches. How cool would that be?" He smiled and politely asked, "What do you have in mind for a budget? Just the wardrobe rental alone will pretty much bankrupt most small towns, let alone the cost of building a small town, Wild West style, that is."

Many no/low budget independent films are written with contemporary, present time settings for good reason. It's going to be difficult converting the modern SUV-laden neighborhood into a pre-WWII era setting complete with vintage-clothed extras and automobiles on a Visa card. It is, for that reason, the present day look with a story line to match is many times the setting for the no/low budget production. Even those concepts can have their fair share of financial challenges. Have you ever wondered why so many no/low budget film productions are in the dark, literally? I'm not referring to just the lighting, or the lack thereof. I'm also referring to the dark story lines. It's the skimpy, non-existent budgets that create films which travel down the road of film noir. The scenes are almost always the same. They all have that same gritty, urban, back alley, stogie-smoking hooker leaning against a dumpster under a streetlamp, look. The reason for the alley, the dumpster and street lamp look? It's settings such as these, which are designed by society, that won't cost a production a ton of money. They can easily be created by anyone; even the hooker, which would only cost you twenty bucks and a six-pack.

Build it and they will come. Great saying, but is it true? No; however, if you have a decent script with easy, logistical locations, it's possible to scrape together enough funds from friends and family to produce a fairly respectable flick. These kinds of scripts are considered to be more of the dialogue-driven stories. They are the kinds of stories that don't require a bunch of high-dollar, special effects to help carry the audience off into the sunset. See for yourself the number of awards that go to the independent films that are nothing more than dialogue-driven screenplays. If there's no money to produce a car chase scene that can rival something from "Gone in Sixty Seconds," why bother? It's only going to come off looking cheesy.

Be real with your expectations when choosing a script. There's much that can be accomplished with good writing, good lighting and good acting; that is, if you are prepared to do the work. In other words, you need a pre-production strategy that rocks.

So, when does pre-production begin? Pre-production begins the minute it is decided that a script-in-hand is soon to become a movie-in-hand. Relinquish yourself to the fact that the project is going to take lots of work, lots of planning and bringing on as many experienced people as possible.

Breaking Down the Script

After a script has been chosen, performing a comprehensive script breakdown is one of the very first steps in the pre-production process. This is where, on paper, and in great detail, everything from actors, crew, wardrobe, props, locations, and times of day for filming are meticulously laid out scene by scene in neat, easy to understand, color coded columns. The script breakdown is not only the key to developing a realistic schedule, but is also the cornerstone for calculating the budget.

The script breakdown process is when the schedule really begins taking shape. How many total days of principal photography will the project require? How many days a week and how many pages per day will be accomplished? How many individuals will be on the set at any given time? How much food will be required on any given day? What special effects, if any, will be required and on what days? What set/production-design preparations will be required? Are there any picture cars, private property buildings, city structures, private roads, city streets and any other property involved with the story that will need to be secured?

The Producer and the Hiring of the Crew

Once the script is in hand and assuming the director is already at the helm, which is usually the case in no/low budget films, the next thing on the to-do list is to hire the producer. This is the person or persons that will hire the crew, make any necessary connections for distribution, book a "B" list actor or two, and help secure financing. Not too many years ago, it was the producer who was the big cheese, the one in charge; however, these days, that role has since shifted more towards the director. In the no/low budget film making world of today, the producer is more inclined to take his or her directions from the director, where in the past, it was just the opposite. Nowadays it is common for the director to have evolved from the writer's role. This makes that person the captain of the ship, so to speak. Notwithstanding, the producer role is not one to take sitting down, no pun intended. In no/low budget filmmaking, the producer is responsible for making sure that things run smoothly and as productively as possible. In other words, his or her job is to produce.

A total dedication to the preparation process should be the producer's ultimate goal. Here's a big warning though; there are many producer wannabe's who are caught up in the glamour of movie making only. They have little interest in taking on the very laborious producer tasks at hand. It's as if they're in it to play the part of moviemaker, much like the way a little girl plays house, providing nothing truly valuable when it comes to actually making a flick. They flaunt their roles only to impress. These types of so-called producers are useless, and frankly, nothing but a cancer to every production they come in contact with. This is a business that requires much hard work from everyone. If a project goes over budget, over schedule and looks like you know what, one doesn't have to look much farther than the producer. A good producer always has a love and a passion for the art of movie making first. They are as concerned with the creative process as the director. Make no concessions; a good producer will indeed secure a most excellent experience.

It is common in the no/low budget film biz, for a director, who is also the writer, to step into the role of producer for a time. This is a hat that the director should only wear temporarily during the very beginning of the pre-production process; only long enough to get a few things set in place. Then the director can pass the torch, so that he or she is able to concentrate on the task at hand.

The UPM

The UPM position is as important as food. Having an experienced UPM on the production team as soon as possible will not only save time, but also save precious dollars. The Unit Production Manager has the responsibilities of overseeing the budget, the script breakdown and putting together a realistic schedule that can be easily followed.

For the "Under the Walnut Tree" production, there was no UPM, at least one who was ever visibly in action. Again, this is the person who makes the schedule, oversees the schedule and sees to it that everyone has said schedule. In the case of this production, the UPM had been fired and replaced by the producer. This was done all in the name of saving a buck. The producer thought he could perform the duties of UPM as well his own. Maybe the original UPM was not working out. If that were the case, the person in the UPM role should have been replaced. Getting rid of that position altogether was just plain insane. The UPM is the one individual who knows, or should know, the inner workings of scheduling and all day-to-day production requirements. This individual is as important to a film production as the camera is to the production.

There are a few positions and departments that can afford to cut a corner or two for the sake of budget; however, the UPM position is not one of them. A good UPM who takes a knowledgeable approach to all aspects of the film making process will help guarantee the production is a success. Whether or not the film fails at the festival, the video store or the box office, I've never heard of it being the fault of the UPM; however, the UPM's failure to meet the day-to-day scheduling and budgetary requirements can certainly doom the project. It just happens long before the project finishes.

The original UPM for the "Under the Walnut Tree" production initially scheduled the film to be shot in ten days at an astounding ten pages per day. This may have looked doable on paper; however, it left no room for anything going wrong whatsoever. Scheduling a film is an intricate dance of time, seasons, personnel, personalities and logistics. It is a job like none other. The UPM must have the organizational skills like the CEO of a large corporation and the psychological prowess of a clinical psychologist. He or she is as valuable to the production as is an engine is to an airplane.

I worked with a so-called producer/writer/director lady many years ago that would actually write the script in her car on the way to the set. That was another fiasco production that failed miserably. It was a production that involved ten-year-old to twelve-year-old children. Because of her lack of scheduling skills and the fact that the production didn't have a UPM, the movie took more than thirteen months to shoot. Little girls who began the project became young women at production's end. Obviously the movie never got finished, big surprise.

Co-Writer/Co-Director

It is common for a first-time screenwriter to desire to wear the director's hat as well. The reason for this is that selling a script, right out of the gate, is many times more difficult than just producing the thing themselves. What happens when there are co-writers conspiring together to make a film? Now instead of just one writer/director, there are at least two individuals, who may find themselves battling for the director's chair.

The co-writer/co-director team is then established. The old adage, two heads are better than one, is the premise. Does this guarantee a smooth production? No. In fact, when the directing team is divided, which is bound to happen at some point, disagreements over the creative process and who's running the show is usually the beginning of an ugly end. Although, there are many writer/director teams who have made it big in motion pictures. The reason for their success is that they created, right from the start, a defining line between the two roles and it is a line that is never crossed. They established how creative differences were going to be addressed, and who was actually going to give the orders. A team approach can work as long as unyielding rules of engagement are securely set in place from the very beginning.

A short film I worked on many years ago turned out to be an absolute calamity. There were more directors than cast and crew. Everyone seemed to be in charge and it was an absolute free for all.

There were arguments about everything, right down to what flavor of gum to have on the craft service table. There's only one director, one captain of the ship. The film production process is a dictatorship, not a democracy.

If you are setting out to co-collaborate on a film project, decide right from the start who is doing what and who is in charge of what. The writer/director for the "Under the Walnut Tree" production and I have been discussing the co-collaboration on a project here in the not-to-distant future. From the very start we've drawn lines in the sand. I have my duties and he has his duties. He brings to the table the creative direction of talent and I bring the creative visual. Do we cross into each other's field of expertise? Of course we do, but only for support and creative input. The final say goes to the department each is responsible for. Collaboration can be a lot of fun and a Godsend when it comes to sharing responsibilities. Just make sure it's clear who's responsible for what.

Choosing the Perfect Director

If you are a writer desiring to transform your work into a movie, but don't wish to take on the task of directing, you'll, no doubt, be seeking a director. This too can be a challenge; finding someone who sees things the way you do. Since the director, for all intents and purposes, is in charge, he or she has the discretion to do with the script what he or she sees fit, even if that suggests re-telling the story in a completely different way. Does that mean someone may want you to rewrite the entire story? Maybe. This is probably the hardest thing for a writer to deal with. If the director is Spielberg, by all means, go for it. He can change anything he wants. If, on the other hand, it's Uncle Herb, he may succumb to a much earlier than expected death. Turning the reigns over to someone else only to have him or her demand a ton of rewrites, is the reason so many writers take on the task of directing their own work.

If you're a screenplay writer and you've, indeed, decided to direct your own work, take the directing role very seriously. It requires a great deal of skill, psychological awareness, hard work and proper execution. I have a chapter just up ahead that's specific to the art of directing; however, it's going to take more than just a chapter in some book to truly get a handle on the task at hand. Learn from those who are successful. Follow their tips, suggestions and experiences. There are plenty of books on the subject and I'd suggest getting a head start on learning the ins and outs of the craft.

Too Many Hats… Not Enough Heads

As I've said before, making any movie, big or small, is a great undertaking which takes discipline, lots of hard work and plenty of experienced people. Entering into the game with half of a team can be a recipe for disaster. A DP, who is also the gaffer and key grip and in charge of props and wardrobe and craft services, when he or she is not planning the lunch menu, is a person who's obviously spreading him or herself way too thin. Of course the preceding is a facetious example; however, it is not too far off the path of reality. This kind of pervasive departmental-sharing mentality is often the approach to crewing for the average no/low budget production.

After the script breakdown, assembling the crew is the next step in the pre-production phase. It is at this time that preliminary key positions are brought into the fold. This group usually includes the Director, if not already established, the DP, Gaffer, Key Grip, Sound Department, Production Designer, Script Supervisor, Make-up/ Wardrobe, Location Scout and D.I.T. (Digital Imaging Tech). These are the basic positions that need to be filled in order to accomplish a realistic pre-production. It is ridiculous to think that any one of these positions can be shared by another department, except for maybe one, which would be the location scout. For those of you with a professional background in the industry, you are probably thinking I'm nuts for saying that; however, in the no-low budget world of filmmaking, there are very seldom funds for such a position. If that is, indeed, the case, it would require all other key positions to be present during the scouting process.

The bottom line is this: hire as many experienced key positions as possible. It will be money spent well. If co-writing/ co-directing is the plan, spend time ironing out any differences during the pre-production phase. It will be time well invested.

Success starts with having the right tool for the job

Chapter Three

LOCATION LOGISTICS and the TECH SCOUT

Location scouting is the part of the pre-production phase that determines which locations work and which locations don't. For the no-low budget bunch, the location scouting process and the tech scouting process may occur simultaneously and may be quite extensive. Nonetheless, it must be done for each and every location.

Before attempting to pursue any part of the scheduling process, it is imperative to take a close look at all logistical aspects of the production first. Logistics play a very important role in the making of any film, whether it's the no-low budget weekend wonder film, or the big Hollywood production. Yet this vital factor is one that is so many times either overlooked or dismissed with the "we'll make it work" approach. Failing to consider simple logistics as a major part of the location seeking process simply ranks right up there with pure insanity. Not once, not twice, but dozens of times, I've encountered the absolute disregard to this very important detail "and it never ends well."

Tech Scouting

For those of you who are not savvy about what tech scouting entails, please allow me to elaborate. Tech scouting or "Technical Scouting" is exactly what it sounds like. This is the time set aside for all related department heads to investigate and scrutinize, with a fine-toothed comb, each location and how it affects their individual departments. For the director, its relevance will hinge on appearance and how the story will be best told in that particular setting. The art department or set decoration, which is usually under the head of the production designer, will take notes from the director and deliver everything necessary to give that location the desired appearance for the scene. The DP, again working with the director, will look for the best camera angles and how they'll match the storyboards. The DP will also determine the overall lighting scheme and what lighting instruments he or she will require. At this time the gaffer will determine what electrical distribution best fits the location. Whether it's the need of a generator, tie-in or simple house power, the gaffer will work in direct concert with the DP to determine the best lighting package for said location, and what will be the best way to provide that electrical power. Note: This is a very important task for no/low budget. The UPM is also along for the ride to take notes, get contact information, and basically get the ball rolling so the location will be ready for principal photography on the day or days scheduled.

I cannot tell you how many times I, as the gaffer, have been brought onto a project after the tech scouting process, in other words, after the locations have already been chosen. Remember, in no/low budget there are no 900-amp generators that power a cornucopia of lighting instruments sitting neatly on a forty-foot trailer. We're not like the big boy productions that come to the party with every motion picture-making piece of equipment ever made. Tech scouting the location is especially important for those of us who don't have all of the cool toys to play with.

Carefully scrutinizing every angle and every scenario for *every* location, scene and set-up should be at the forefront of the pre-production process. The following is the logistical approach to the tech scout procedure, and what the production team should be looking for.

Location Logistics

Again, if you don't have it in the budget to hire a trained professional Location Scout, "ALL" department heads must be involved with the location scouting process. Many times in the no-low budget realm, the director, writer and producer, along with a doobie or two, will take off to find a few of the main locations all by themselves, as though they're on some happy-go-lucky field trip. Then after the fact, they bring a few of the department heads along for a tech scout to "make it work." The problem with that kind of approach is they may get all excited about "the look" of a particular location and disregard any logistics that would be involved. This approach does nothing for the production. When property is scheduled that doesn't work, or at the very least work well, it ultimately results in spending big bucks that can't be afforded.

All mega Hollywood productions consider logistics for every shot they plan. The difference is, they can afford to "make it work." Street closures? No problem. Need more lights? No problem. And if the interior doesn't quite work, recreate it on a sound stage. As mentioned before, the no/low budget independent film is many times more difficult to produce than a big budget film, from the logistical standpoint that is. Observe the credits at the end of any major Hollywood film, and see for yourself the multitudes of personnel it takes to bring a film production to fruition. While in the no/low budget world, there's an entire crew of three; all of who scramble around the set like crazed fire ants trying to place a single C-stand. Just that scenario alone should give credence to the fact that a logistical plan of attack is a must for the no/low budget bunch.

Many times, during the "Under the Walnut Tree" production, we were scheduled to shoot at a location we had never seen before, the following day. That meant that key individuals such as the DP, gaffer, sound department and even the director, had never stepped one foot onto the location prior to the scheduled shoot day. We would find ourselves spending the first two to three hours vying for parking spots, trying to find suitable staging areas, searching for lighting placement locations, power supply options, camera angles and whatever else was blindly handed to us that day. At the time, the only concern on the table was…can the location be acquired for free?

Logistical Noise

So, what's to consider first when logistically choosing a location? This question is as perplexing as what came first, the chicken or the egg? The location could be perfect in all aspects with great looks, plenty of parking and plenty of electrical power, but if the location is fifty feet from railroad tracks, is it going to work? Expanding on this scenario a bit, consider the logistical aspects, and ask the right questions. Train tracks fifty feet away may be okay for some scenes, but if this is a location where a large majority of the movie is going to be filmed and trains are passing by every fifteen minutes, the location is obviously not going to work. If, however, the railroad tracks are abandoned or they're a short service spur line and they are hardly ever used, then the location may indeed work. How long does the production plan on occupying said location? If only for a couple of days and sound isn't a huge issue, maybe the production will benefit just fine setting up camp there. Noise issues are a big deal. Whether its planes, trains or automobiles, the noise factor must always be at the top of the list of concerns for any location, unless of course it's a silent movie you're filming.

Several years ago I worked on a short film in Washington that used a small, out-of- the-way lake for its backdrop. Once again, I cannot stress enough the importance of a stringent location tech scout. This lake turned out to be the worst location ever for shooting anything that required sound recording. The lake was, indeed, the picturesque setting ideal for the film, save for one small detail. At the south end of the lake, there was a VOR beacon directing all north and south aircraft traffic to and from the Portland Oregon International Airport.

It was one sound bust after another as plane after plane flew over at five hundred feet directly above. Planes, trains and automobiles are a way of life unless you're filming on another planet. Be cognizant of all surroundings. Know the location environment implicitly. Expect to spend some serious time considering sound-recording issues connected with a particular location.

A Camping Trip

While actually filming under the big walnut tree, even though we were miles from anywhere remotely resembling civilization, the non-stop noise literally killed take after take. There were farm tractors, trains, dump trucks and planes passing by or overhead every five minutes, day after day. What should have taken eight days to shoot took an entire month. If only a camping trip had taken place, things might have been different.

Time consuming as it may seem, making a camping trip out of a location tech scout is certainly one way to observe the surroundings of a location and all of the idiosyncrasies. Planning an overnight expedition at the "Under the Walnut Tree" location for a full 24-hour cycle would have exposed many, if not all, issues that would come to plague the filming schedule.

The sound department would have known, well in advance, about all of all of the planes, trains and automobiles that created sound issues every thirty minutes. The Director and DP would have been aware of how long a shoot day to expect given the earlier than normal sunset, due to the dense tree cover. Had there been a UPM, he or she would have planned accordingly to prevent filming during the time the leaves began falling off the trees. Does this suggest they should have found another location? Maybe, but not necessarily. Adjusting the schedule to accommodate the many inhibiting factors may have been the only requirement. The point being, principal photography is not the time to realize the feasibility factors of a particular location.

Logistical Coordinates

Due to the fact that a majority of the productions I work on take place around the 45th parallel in the Pacific Northwest, there are inherent seasonal and weather related issues that must always be considered top priority. It is no secret we have our fair share of rain. That being said, if a particular production up here is to have a sunny, summer setting, there are only about two-and-a-half to three months during the year to film such a project. This brings up another logistical issue. Because we are at the 45th parallel, days are very long during the summer months and consequently the nights are very short; which makes the opposite true during the winter months. Since a production day is typically ten hours, night filming here in the Pacific Northwest during the summer months, only provides seven hours of darkness. The same must be taken into consideration for wintertime filming. The winter days are very short, and if the story revolves around those months, any day filming will be much shorter as well. A logistical approach to scheduling the shorter days or shorter nights must be considered.

This was the issue during the "Under the Walnut Tree" production. Many of the scenes were to take place at the "walnut tree"; exterior days and exterior nights. Because we were filming at the tail end of the summer months, we only had a fraction of the ten-hour production day to achieve all of the night scenes. Due to the fact that the major part of the story takes place under the walnut tree, it would have been best for principal photography to have started a couple of weeks earlier. This would have guaranteed more time to complete all of the scenes under said tree before the season of non-stop rain and de-leafing of all foliage would set in. Latitudinal and longitudinal coordinates play a huge role in the proper planning and scheduling for any motion picture. Not only do geographical locations affect predominate weather, they also affect the lighting in terms of how long and where the sun will or will not be at any given time.

Logistics of the Sun

How will the direction and travel of the sun affect a film production? Due to the lack of finances for the no/low budget bunch, there are typically no powerful lighting instruments or large grip packages that help to combat the many effects of the big orange ball in the sky. These undeniable issues dictate the importance of knowing the direction and horizontal situation of the sun's travel at all times. That being said, it is also important that the placement of buildings, or the structural compass headings of said buildings within a scene, be considered when logistically planning a production.

The "Under the Walnut Tree" production had secured an apartment complex to use as the lead actress's home. Unfortunately, this was done without any discussion with the departments that would be directly affected by any logistic ramifications of using that particular property.

Jill's apartment was a setting that was surrounded by debauchery, drugs and loathing, which was her life prior to her abduction. The drug-ridden complex and the dilapidated apartment was the perfect setting, save for the fact that the complex was situated at the end of the local airport's runway 34 left, (air traffic). Jill, our lead character's apartment also faced east and west. To the untrained eye, this would have not been much of a concern; however, the look of the building was, once again, the only factor that dictated the decision making process in securing this location. Logistics had the building facing the wrong way, geographically. This decision meant the sun track, along with the building's geographical placement, would determine at which time during the day certain angles within the apartment could take place.

The front door of our character's apartment faced west. This meant there was plenty of sunlight pouring in through the front windows during the mid to late afternoon; however, it was just the opposite during the morning hours. The low-laying sun during morning hours, meant sunlight came in through the east-facing back bedroom windows. The time of day and the amount of time we had to shoot a scene was always at the forefront of the day's schedule. Due to the sun's position in the sky, in relation to the geographic placement of the complex, it created lighting and scheduling issues that were always difficult to work with.

Anyone, who's been in the movie making business for any length of time will agree that recreating sunlight is easy, if the production is financially blessed; however, trying to replace sunlight with a small1200 PAR HMI is equivalent to lighting a nighttime football game with a street lamp. There are only three choices; block out the sun and replace it with big powerful lighting instruments, reflect the sunlight into the scene and work quickly, or film at a location that takes into consideration all situational awareness aspects. In other words, consider logistics.

Within the world of the no/low budget independent film making process, there will always be a lack of lighting instruments and lack of textiles designed to control sunlight. It was no easy task extending the day on the west side of the apartment complex, considering that the best light we had, after the sun went behind the adjacent building, was two1200 PAR HMIs. This was hardly the replacement sun necessary to match earlier ambient f-stops. If the apartment complex would have had a north/south geographical facing placement instead, this would not have been an issue.

The Logistics of Power

It's no secret, having a grip and lighting package that runs on two semi trailers and a ten-ton truck is one of the greatest dreams for any film production. On the other hand, the lack of said grip and lighting instruments and doodads will do nothing but zap the crap out of any desired creative input. What's even more frustrating is having all of the lighting instruments one could wish for, but not having enough electrical power to operate them.

The no/low budget independent film production usually doesn't have the money to rent huge power plants (generators) to haul around from location to location. This lack of power means that locations have sufficient house power, straight off the grid, to handle all of the production's demands. When working in most buildings, whether an apartment, house or office complex, the best one can usually expect to have available for electrical power is a couple-hundred amps. This is not much, but it's certainly doable if a proper production design plan has been implemented. The key is, once again, the tech scout. Has the proper inspection of available electrical power, indeed, taken place?

Several years back, while working on one of those so-called weekend wonder films, the writer/director, at the last minute, was able to schedule an old farmhouse to be used for a couple of small scenes. The scenes required both night interiors and night exteriors; however, they could both easily be shot in ten hours or less. He immediately sent word out to the cast and crew that the call time was scheduled for 3:00 PM that very day. This was one of those locations he had been seeking to land from Day One, but had been unable to secure until one day prior to actually filming. This means, of course, that there had been no time to accomplish a proper location tech scout on the farmhouse. Knowing we didn't have a generator scheduled, house power had to be the sole source of electricity. He simply had no choice but to assume there was plenty of electrical power to run all of the lighting instruments, including all of the other departmental needs.

At the scheduled call time, we all arrived and began the unloading and staging process. When the director arrived, he promptly unlocked the front door and we all entered. What we saw made our hair stand up on end. The wiring was from some time around the 1920s or 30s. The asbestos-insulated wires were mounted to the outside of the interior walls via porcelain insulators. The Edison plug-in receptacles were grounded, non-polarized, two-pronged electrocution boxes. The fuse box was in the basement, hosting only four fuses; two 10-amp fuses designated to the main floor, and two 10-amp fuses for the second floor. It was nothing but a 2,000 square-foot fire bomb. Just one 2K light alone could have set the place ablaze. Referring to a family photo on the old oak end table at the end of the couch, I asked, "Are these the people who live here?" The gentleman and his wife were easily in their mid-to-late eighties and had lived there since their wedding day. These people probably thought they were living on the cutting edge of technology simply because they weren't using oil lamps.

The electrical distribution concerns for any location will always be at the top of the list when it comes to logistics, especially when it comes to the no/low budget independent film project. Very seldom will a power plant be available for those of us film pirates who plunder locations much like a run-amuck traveling stage show. That being said, make absolutely sure there is sufficient and safe house power to be able to handle the electrical demands. There is more on the subject of electrical distribution in part two.

The Logistics of Access

Accessibility and adequate space to perform the duties of filmmaking are essential to the success of any production, big or small. Sets located on a Hollywood sound stage have plenty of room for movie making. That's what they're designed for. The sound stage provides a quiet, controlled environment in which to shoot with plenty of space and easy access. There is power beyond expectation and a cafeteria within walking distance. In contrast, the no/low budget bunch must suffer noisy, off the wall locations, cold pepperoni pizza, lukewarm coffee, and a tiny, single-burner propane camp heater for all to huddle around.

Accessibility and space are often so overlooked it's almost comedic. What good is it to land a location that no one can get to or shoot in, for whatever reasons? Our make-up lady for the "Under the Walnut Tree" production had stumbled onto a location that she thought would be perfect for an interior nightclub scene. Forty-five miles later, on a Friday night, twelve of us from the production team stormed the small downtown club like a wedding party gone awry. Again, it was one of those last minute location scout escapades.

While she was just trying to help, she didn't exactly know what she needed to be looking for; yet we all followed along as though we were cattle being led to slaughter. Why anyone would think the make-up lady would have sufficient knowledge of how to properly perform a location scout falls very short of rational thinking. It's about as absurd as having the night manager at Taco Bell command the next space shuttle mission. Nice try, but no cigar.

The club was located on the corner of a one-way downtown street. The town had a population of approximately 5,000. Even though the town was small, the club was considered to be more of an upscale, classy establishment, which was exactly what the director was looking for, save for the fact, the size of the club. Measuring maybe eighteen feet wide and seventy-five feet long, it was nothing more than a bowling alley with cloth-covered tables. There was absolutely no room for grip equipment, lighting instruments and no place for crew and actors to work. There were full-sized windows that graced the entire length of the club on one side, which would have forced us into filming during nighttime hours only. The bottom line was this particular establishment was not going to work. Lesson learned: all location scouting should be performed long before principal photography begins.

One project I had worked on a few years back had chosen one of their locations to be in a less-than-ideal part of the city. The brick building was one-hundred-plus years old with no power and as creepy as an honest-to-goodness haunted house. Parking within six blocks of the location was all but non-existent. The fourth floor, where the scene took place, had no elevator and only a narrow winding staircase to transport everything our trucks had to offer, which included a four-hundred-plus pound Fisher Ten camera dolly, complete with all associated hardware and six lengths of track. At first glance, another more accessible location would have been the first consideration; however, every attention to detail had been thought of well in advance, including the amount of labor required to make it all happen.

During the tech scout phase, with all appropriate department heads present, it was apparent that it would take many hands to move equipment, props, and furnishings from the trucks to the fourth floor. A production designer and his crew would be hired very early on to design and build the interior sets and ready to go by the first day of principal photography. Also, it was determined that parking permits, along with street closure permits, would be required for the eleven days scheduled at that location. The lighting package included two 4K HMIs, two man-lifts, four 1200 PAR HMIs, and a good-sized tungsten package, all of which would be powered by a 900-amp generator complete with all of the necessary cables and distribution boxes to properly light the fourth-floor set. Because rain was an intricate part of the story, hydrant permits and rain towers were also required. Any and all pre-rigging and de-rigging time was also factored in. This added an additional four days to the seven days of principal photography.

Meticulous planning not only assured plenty of help for all of the heavy work, it also guaranteed there would be plenty of parking for cast and crew. Also factored in was plenty of space for craft services, a catering tent, and a combination wardrobe/make-up truck, complete with two honey wagons and a production office motorhome. The location resembled nothing less than a big budget film-set, yet this was a very low budget film. The trick to making it all happen on such a low budget was pre-production planning. They utilized the one-day rental option for grip and lighting equipment and they deferred as many of the costs as possible. Even though the movie was written as a feature length, much of the entire budget was dedicated to that one location. There was absolutely nothing left to chance. The remaining scenes were all achieved using nothing more than a skeleton crew, sack lunches and a couple of small lighting instruments. From the beginning, everyone knew exactly how and what was going on. There were storyboards, schedules and shot lists that were followed to a tee. In most cases, the four-story downtown location would have been all but impossible to use given the meager budget; however, a solid make-it-happen, well-planned strategy was implemented right from the start. This approach not only guaranteed that particular location would be a success, but that the entire production would be a success. Strategic, logistical planning made what would have been impossible, possible.

Logistics of Guerilla Filming

Guerilla: As in guerilla warfare – Clandestine, secretive - To film on location without permits or permission - Illegal trespassing.

The "Under the Walnut Tree" producer presented to us an urban, back alley location that, at face value, should have worked out just fine and if only ten minutes of tech scout had been performed, it too would not have turned into a huge disaster. The particular scene took place with our lead actress walking down a deserted alleyway at night. She had just been thrown out of a nightclub for drunken, insidious behavior, only to have an encounter with her soon-to-be abductor. The scene had her abductor slowly driving up behind her in the alley in his pickup truck at which time she was grabbed, chloroformed, and taken away into the night.

Once again, the alley was one of those last minute location grabs; no permits, no logistical forethought as to whether the alley would even work. Borrowing power from a local business with a single extension cord exiting from the back door was all that was available when it came to electricity. A1200 PAR HMI, a 300-watt Fresnel and a 42-inch monitor was all we could power from the single plug-in. To make things worse, the background bar our actress got thrown from closed at 11:00 PM sharp, which meant that our background flashing neon lighting went dark as well. During that particular time of year, late September early October, the sun doesn't completely set till around 8pm. That gave us a whole whopping three hours to film a scene that would easily take eight hours.

There is an old saying, "Choose your battles wisely." These are words to live by when working in no/low budget filmmaking. Had this been properly scouted in advance, we would have been just fine; the alley scene should have been scheduled as an eight-hour night with a complete alley closure. There was no regard given to acquiring a simple fifty-dollar permit. It was assumed, incorrectly, that the "guerilla" approach to filmmaking should have worked for this particular location.

Only for a few short, well-planned scenes does the guerrilla approach to filmmaking ever work. Unfortunately for most attempts, it ends up being hard labor, all for nothing. Frankly, with some of our cities going permit crazy, it's easy to see why the guerrilla shoot continues to be a staple within the no/low budget independent filmmaking society. In fact, they're the shots that will stimulate coffee talk for many years thereafter. I liken it to the streaking fad of the late sixties and early seventies; running through a Denny's parking lot, stark naked on a Friday night, after the big game. There's nothing like the adrenaline rush one gets when attempting to grab the shot of the black sedan driving by while actors point prop machine gun barrels out of back windows during rush hour traffic. After all, it's about realism, right?

Several years back, while working with a director friend of mine, we had made the unfortunate decision to film a scene alongside a reflecting pool located at a local college, a very prestigious college at that. Getting to the reflecting pool required us to hike a good quarter of a mile down a path of steps and landings approximately three-hundred feet lower in elevation. If we had only needed to carry a tiny handy-cam and a flex-fill, it would not have turned into the aerobic event that it did. Making sure we were able to get the "cool" shots, we packed, down to the reflecting pool, our eighteen-foot Jimmy Jib along with the 200-plus pounds of weights, shiny boards, combo stands and, of course, a monitor or two. Why is it that when performing the big "guerrilla shoot", the police don't show up until everything is set up and ready for the first shot? Needless to say, we were forced to tear everything down and pack it all out without even rolling one inch of footage.

Every time I hear from production that we're going to "guerrilla the shot", my blood runs cold. In some towns it's as easy as buying a fake Rolex from a New York City street vendor; whereas in towns like Los Angeles, it's twenty-five to life in San Quentin. Please understand, I'm neither discouraging nor promoting the guerrilla approach to filmmaking. I believe when it comes to no/low budget, all is fair game at one time or another; however, simple logistical questions still must be asked. Can the guerrilla shot be done quickly and easily, and if the shot does fail because the police show up, how detrimental will it be to the film? In other words, how much time and energy will be wasted? As exciting as the guerrilla shot is, there are consequences and is the production willing to except those consequences? I think this may be the only time where a vote among key departments would be acceptable. All department heads involved must either agree or disagree to the work, risks, and consequences.

For those of us who work outside the convenience of the Hollywood studio, the world becomes our stage. That responsibility demands that we spend even more time factoring in every logistical angle, feasible practicality, and legal ramification.

A final note: Because the film permit process varies from town to town, I suggest first checking with your local city hall; however, this will only be necessary if considering the use of city streets, public sidewalks and parks, in other words, any place you feel you and your band of movie making renegades are unable to outrun the cops.

"If the world is my stage, I want better lighting"

Chapter Four

SCHEDULING

Effective scheduling ultimately determines the success of a project on so many levels. Not only is it a determining factor when it comes to quota and budget, it also determines overall morale for both cast and crew. The aggressive, ten-pages-a-day for ten straight days schedule, is certainly one way to shoot a no/low budget indie film, but is it realistic? I think the bigger question is: what will be the ultimate outcome? Does the film really have the quality one would be proud to put his or her name on? Or does the film do nothing more than provide a few days of pay, along with a few slices of cold pizza? Perhaps the more important question would be: are we satisfied with just having a gig, or are we in this business for the creative aspects and expression? I think it's important to understand that scheduling, in its totality, is a complex component in production involving many factors that not only include money, personalities and logistics, but creativity as well. Before stepping too far into the overtly fastidious task of scheduling, we must first understand what is considered a normal production day.

The Ten Hour Production Day

The unions, SAG (Screen Actors Guild) and I.A.T.S.E. (International Alliance of Theatrical Stage Employees) consider a production day to be ten hours, including a thirty-minute break for lunch (Hot Meal). This does not mean that the lights go out, and everyone punches a clock and walks off the set at the end of ten hours. For union pictures, ten hours is when overtime begins. The average daily schedule is approximately twelve to fifteen hours and that's for productions that run a fairly tight ship. Sadly, in no/low budget terms, ten hours often implies things are just getting started. The reasons for many of the scheduling snafus for no/low budget projects come down to a myriad of factors. Many of those factors are simple and easy fixes, but due to lack of experience, they are simply not considered. The ten-hour production day, for the most part, is a luxury for any film production, let alone the proverbial weekend wonder film. For no/low budget film productions, the cast and crew are often hired and paid a specific flat rate in dollars and cents. Either they are paid a daily rate, weekly rate, or run of show rate. Unfortunately, this type of flat rate pay structure allows for a lot of labor abuse; hence, the eighteen-hour production day for ten hours of pay.

As we delve deeper into the mechanics of film making, it'll become clear how to ascertain and follow a workable schedule; one that can be appreciated by all who are aboard. Probably the biggest complaint on-set is the hunger factor. If you've ever held what would be considered a regular day job, the lunch break begins at about four hours or half way into the shift; however, in the film world we must wait a bit longer

Hot Meal/Lunch

The thirty minute break for lunch or "Hot Meal" begins no earlier and no later than six hours from the call time. The six-hour lunch clock is based on the more typically longer twelve-hour production day, in other words, about half way into the shift. The thirty-minute clock begins when the last person goes through the catering line. If you're the first person through, you have a longer lunch period. It's typical for the producers, director, DP and keys to go through the line first, then the crew, and last but not least, the actors. This practice gives key individuals time for brief meetings that would normally distract from the actual filming schedule, and also ensures that the crew is back on set with lights up and ready for talent when their lunch is over. There is an exception to the six-hour rule and that is when "Grace" has been called. Grace is a term that is used by the director. He or she is requesting more time to finish a shot that is currently in progress before breaking for lunch. The Grace rule states the camera cannot move or change position unless, of course, they're conducting a dolly shot. Grace is ultimately designed for the actor or actors. It allows them extra time to finish their scene, so that they can remain in character before breaking for lunch; however, there are financial meal penalties for going too long past the six-hour limit. For the major motion picture world, making "union sanctioned type films", penalty moneys can quickly add up. In the no/low budget world; however, these union lunch rules are not always followed as closely.

As I looked over the call sheet on the first day of principal photography for the "Under the Walnut Tree production", I noticed that the first hot meal lunch break was way down at the bottom of the page. Someone had us working nine consecutive hours before the first Hot Meal. That was quickly revised.

I'm often asked, how many pages per day should be expected for a typical principal photography schedule? This is like asking, how many pairs of socks should one own? Realistically speaking, there are simply too many variables and factors that must be considered.

Four Pages per Day... Fact or Fiction

"How many pages per day?" This is a valid question that should be asked when attempting to develop a viable shooting schedule; however, the answer is all too subjective and deserves careful consideration from many angles. There has been a vague rumor over the years that states four pages a day is the norm. Not true. Consider, for a moment, the following example:

Detective Barrett sits across the street in his unmarked police car. He waits incognito for the bank robbers to exit the front door. As the bank robbers exit the bank, get into the getaway car, and speed off, Detective Barrett starts his car, slams it in gear and speeds off after them. After six or seven blocks of a high-speed chase, Detective Barrett and the getaway car both crash into several parked cars in the mall parking lot. Detective Barrett exits his car and a shootout ensues. Detective Barrett is shot. He immediately falls to the ground and his eyes roll back into his head. He's been killed. The bank robbers smile at each other, dust themselves off and enter into the mall. They enter the food court and enjoy a round of hotdogs, a refreshing soda and reminisce about the day's exciting events.

Depending on the overall production value, the amount of coverage, and of course the budget, the preceding car chase alone could easily take several days to shoot. This hardly follows the four-page-a-day rule. Conversely, there are scenes that require much less coverage. They're usually the scenes that take place in one location with one or two actors. Sometimes there isn't even any dialogue. These are the scenes that rely on the "a picture is worth a thousand words" concept. Scenes such as these could mean smoking through six to ten pages of principal photography in a single day, no problem.

The budget is, no doubt, the first of many issues that will dictate the "how many pages per day" factor. It's the nature of the beast. The lower the budget, the more pages must be shot per day. There's cast and crew to pay and feed, a ton of equipment to be rented, plus dozens of other expenditures. One knee-jerk reaction to keeping the cost down is to shoot ten pages a day for ten days straight. However, as attractive as this may seem on paper, it usually leads to a disastrous outcome.

Over-aggressive scheduling, or cramming, doesn't usually work very well. It means that there's limited time for multiple takes. It also means that there's little time for interesting story-telling visuals, not to mention cast and crew burn out. The fact that this is the performing arts business implies that there must be some creative input involved. If a quality product is the desire, rushing through the production day at near light-speed-pace just for the sake of "getting it in the can" is actually more counter-productive than one would care to believe. Scheduling a production that is going to be successful begins with raising enough money to ensure such an outcome. That may come off as a bit simplistic, but it's usually the reality of it all. Scheduling with a less than desirable budget usually forces a production to accept things that aren't always in the best interest of creativity. For whatever reason, maybe it's the lack of planning or foresight, but it seems to be the no/low budget independent film that has a greater propensity to spend what little money they do have, in all of the wrong places.

Working with a young director, not too long ago, was a bit of a challenge. Because of his particular approach to directing, it took more than the average amount of time to get a take he liked. It was common for him to ask for 15 to 20 takes per set-up. He also had a tendency to get lots of coverage. That would have been fine if the shooting schedule hadn't required a pace of 6 to 8 pages a day. If a director requires numerous takes and lots of coverage, which is his or her prerogative, the schedule will need to be adjusted to accommodate that. This particular production should have scheduled for two to three pages per day, which would have been more realistic.

We've established the fact that the director's approach to directing is an important factor to consider in scheduling. One must also consider some deeper psychological influences that come into play. There is more on the psychological ramifications of a director in chapter eight, but I would like to point out now that experience and confidence play a big part in determining how many pages a production may expect to complete.

There is also the actor factor, which has just as much influence on the flow of a production day as the director. An actor who lacks experience and know-how is a factor that can easily spin a good day bad. Thirty-nine takes because an actor can't remember lines or perform his or her part as required, tears holes in the daily schedule faster than a mouse tears through a piece of Swiss cheese. Again, this is a huge subject that will be discussed later on; however, until then, think rehearsal, rehearsal, and more rehearsal.

There is the factor of the crew to consider as well when discussing the "how many pages per day" controversy. Does the production have well-seasoned professional crewmembers or seventeen-year-old interns? Of course, this reverts back to the obvious budgetary constraint issues discussed earlier. If the budget is such that the seventeen-year-old intern apprenticeship program is the status quo, then it's fair to say set-ups are going to take up a long part of the production day. It usually goes beyond experience though. It also has much to do with the number of crewmembers that are on the set at any given time. One gaffer and two interns does not a crew make, but much of the time, this is the team we have to work with. The one saving grace in this scenario is that typically, the set-ups are not that big for the typical no/low budget independent film. There simply isn't a budget for condor cranes, huge power plants or big lighting set-ups. Still the same, this is just something else that has to be taken into consideration when trying to determine the how-many-pages-per-day factor.

When I think about first getting into the "grip" end of the film making business, one day, in particular, comes to mind. As the token intern I, like many others before and after me, had no idea what I was doing. At one point, the key grip went running by me with things in his hands, yelling for me to fetch three cupblocks and bring them out back behind the building. Cold-blooded horror ran through my veins. The only thing I could think was what is a cupblock? Walking towards the grip truck, I knew I had to come up with something quick. Either I bring something that in my imagination resembles a cupblock back to him or I pretend to forget that he even asked me to fetch him the doodad in the first place. Asking the high exalted one of grippage what a cupblock was, was absolutely out of the question. After all, I didn't want to come off looking like an idiot. As luck would have it, a stake truck from the grip and lighting rental house came to make a delivery at that very moment. Steve, the delivery guy, jumped out of the driver side door and asked me to give him a hand unloading the equipment. I immediately jumped into action giving him the hand he so desperately needed. It was then I contrived my plan to find out what the heck a cupblock was.

"Hey Steve," I asked, "Where are the cupblocks on the grip truck? I can't find them."

"They're where there always at."

This was not the answer I wanted to hear. With a witty retort I said, "No they're not."

After we finished unloading the stake truck, Steve jumped up into the grip truck, walked down the narrow isle toward the front, grabbed the long all-thread hanger of cupblocks and tossed them at me. "Right where I said they were," he said.

"Oh, I guess they were hidden by some other stuff." I tried hard to sound convincing. Steve just walked by me without saying a word. He jumped off the grip truck, climbed back inside the stake truck and sped off. The point I'm making here is that interns don't know things and they can't be expected to know things. As much as I hate for a film project to turn into film school, this is an inevitable fact for the no/low budget scenario. That being said, I make it clear to those who sport lesser knowledge on the set to always ask. If you don't know something, ask. There is neither the time nor the patience for ridiculous guessing games.

Night versus day schedules may not have much to do with the number of pages per day one can expect, but they do affect the overall length of the production and the ever prominent, over-scheduling issue. Try shooting a ten-to- twelve-hour day and then from there go directly into nights without any turnaround time. The crew will, no doubt, have some strong words for that game plan. A day off between the day schedule and the night schedule or "turnaround" as it's referred to, will need to be factored in. The same is true when switching back to days. Turnarounds during principal photography will add days to the overall production schedule and that, of course, is dependent on how many turnarounds there are.

The scheduling, or lack thereof, for the "Under the Walnut Tree" production had us flipping back and forth between days and nights throughout the entire production. Some of this scheduling nightmare was nonsense, and some was totally understandable. While it is true that a production fairs best if all the days are grouped together and the nights are grouped together, the ugly fact of the matter is that this may be impossible. Locations that may require both day and night scenes may only be available for a certain period of time. Flip-flopping between days and nights then becomes the nature of the beast; however, if the scheduling process during the pre-production phase is performed properly, this too should be a rarity.

Backup Plan

"Martini" is a term representing the last shot of the day. The last thing any production needs is for the "Martini" to take place three hours into the schedule, unless of course, it's planned that way. It is essential to the overall schedule to have a backup plan if an early-day wrap occurs. In other words, there must be a plan for "X" amount of pages per day. What's on the back burner if a production day gets cut short for whatever reason? In order for the day to continue, it may be a situation that calls for an alternative location, scene or setup. Time is money for any business and show business is no different.

Some time ago, during an exterior street scene, it began to rain, and rain it did, all day long. The scene required dry streets, dry cars and dry actors since we had shot the connecting set-ups under dry conditions the previous day. The bottom line is, the day was a bust; a total rain out. It didn't take long for the question to arise, now what? There were the obvious, "That's a wrap" comments floating around, and of course the "Let's go to the bar and think about this for awhile" suggestions that came up frequently. The sad fact was there was no backup plan. There was nowhere else to go. We were filming in the Pacific Northwest where one must always expect rain. You'd think a rain plan would have been in someone's back pocket. Instead, eighteen filmmakers were sitting in a bar, knee deep in booze by 1:30 PM.

Having an alternative plan, just in case of such of an event, is a must. What happens if a scene is cut short? Is there anything planned that can be used as a fill-in, just in case? A good UPM who knows how to properly plan ahead, along with a script supervisor who has some forethought about an alternate scene or location, which could be ready to go at the drop of a hat, can many times save the day. It's that kind of progressive planning that keeps the overall "X" number of pages per day on track, which in turn, obviously saves time and money.

"It's not the time it takes to take the take; it's the time between the takes that take the time".

Chapter Five

DISCIPLINED PRACTICES

Over Scheduling

As the eighteenth hour rapidly approaches, it's easy to point the "over scheduling" finger around the set while eating red licorice and peanuts at the craft service table; however, one doesn't have to go far to realize its chronic inception usually spawns from "lack of discipline." Lack of discipline is most common with today's fast-food bunch of digital moviemakers. It's the new-to-industry types who have never worked with what is quickly becoming thought of as the old-fashioned, motion-picture "film-wielding camera".

Obviously, lack of experience is common among the newbie independent filmmakers of today. And, it's the lack of experience that is usually the common denominator when it comes to a cornucopia of long days. Eighteen-hour days do happen, and for the big union pictures that pay the big bucks for overtime, bring it on. For the no/low budget flat rate bunch, eighteen-hour days suck. And worse yet, they're unnecessary for the most part.

A DP friend of mine and I were having a discussion about a scene we had shot a few days prior. The discussion stemmed from the question; what caused the filming of that scene to fail so miserably? In actuality the problem was as obvious as the nose on Pinocchio's face. We were, again, beginning a new scene at the end of an already long day. Everyone was beat-tired and lacking any creative energy whatsoever. Over scheduling was the issue. It was on the schedule to accomplish a certain number of scenes, but the facts were apparent; there were too many pages of script scheduled, given the circumstances. And that, my friend, is the biggest reason productions delve into eighteen-hour days. While minimizing those long grueling days is certainly in the overall production's best interest, it becomes an even greater interest when trying to maintain everyone's sanity.

I'm certainly not suggesting that a production should schedule five-hour shoot days, because the movie would never get done; however, scheduling for ten-to-twelve-hour days and never seeing anything but eighteen-hour days will make the whole team quickly realize something has gone horribly awry. Five questions must be answered when this type of scheduling miscalculation occurs. Were storyboards or shot lists followed, and if not why? Was the director's experience taken into consideration during the planning and scheduling process? Were there any key individuals who came to the party with a background of film-production disciplines? Were there too many intricate complex scenes planned for an already busy day of filming? And lastly, were there too many company moves planned?

Some productions simply don't take into consideration these five factors, which are common causes for falling behind schedule. When things do spin out of control, the days become games of catch-up.

It is fair to say there are some productions that purposely schedule ten days straight at eighteen-hours-per-day. The majority of them are nothing more than task-aggressive, mass production line films. In other words, they've turned the art of movie making into widget making. Just so you know, these are nothing but cookie cutter productions and have no more creative inspiration than a package of Top Ramen. Nine times out of ten, these types of weekend wonder films are written to be down-and-dirty, low dollar smut films. The producers have but one interest; make a fast, cheap movie and sell it oversees for a huge profit that only they enjoy. These types of films are nothing more than flaccid frames of blood, butts and boobs entwined with a storyline that's as weak as a ninety- year-old cancer patient. One step this side of porn, they're hardly the great creative Academy-award winning works of art the majority of us got into this business to produce.

Even though they're challenging, when independent films are written and produced properly, they're always inspiring, and for the most part, fun to work on. They fuel the filmmaker in all of us. There's nothing sweeter than successfully completing a scene that has the makings of an award winning, cinematic work of art. When creativity is flowing heavily and there's that special energy in the air that guarantees you'll get something really cool in the can, no one will ever complain about a long day.

At the opposite end of the production scale, we find those works of art that are not yet seasoned with experience. They kind of know where they are headed and what they want, but they're not quite there yet. These types of productions bring a whole new meaning to the word discipline. They're the productions that don't quite think things through. Instead they run on aggressive excitement only and it's obvious they are thwarted and stalled by lack of experience and lack of planning. Their only recourse is to over-shoot the crap out of every single scene. They desperately hope something interestingly usable jumps in front of the lens and wiggles.

Shooting Ratio Disciplines

Back in the day when no/low budget independent films were actually shot on "film", too much coverage was never an issue. It was and still is today way too expensive, and for the very low budget productions, out of the question all together. For the digital age of today we see directors and DPs covering scenes like never before. Although still expensive, it's just not realized in terms of film purchase. So we must ask ourselves, why do we need to cover the application of lipstick twenty-six different ways to Sunday? I liken the "over-coverage" scenario to credit card purchases. Since there's no real, hard cash being pulled from the wallet at the time, the purchase doesn't appear too painful. Just like with the credit card purchase, the bill will come due and the real expense of "over coverage" will be realized at the end of the production.

A seasoned director, who has come through the ranks of shooting on film, whether 16mm or 35mm, understands the disciplines of the shooting ratio. The shooting ratio is easily determined by how many takes there are prior to the director calling out. "That's a print." These are words not heard in today's digital no/low budget independent movie making world. This term means they would like a particular portion of film developed as a work print and sent back to them in the form of dailies. In other words, the captured footage must be developed and sent back to the production so it can be viewed to verify the footage is indeed going to work. The amount of feet of film that passes through the gate for any given set-up is of serious budgetary concern. It's this factor that determines the shooting ratio for a particular scene or set-up. If it requires four hundred feet of film to capture one hundred feet of usable footage, it equates to a four-to-one (4:1) shooting ratio.

A long time director friend of mine made an interesting observation: the young directors of today are simply not disciplined. They were not brought up in the industry with yesterday's budgetary concerns of dealing with the cost of actual film. They dismiss take after take as if there is no end to time.

Along with the hypothetical rule of four pages per day, there is also the (4:1) shooting ratio goal that is applied when shooting on film. If you're wondering whether the (4:1) shooting ratio is set in stone, the answer is no. I would have to say in my experience, depending on the budget, (10:1) is closer to the actual shooting ratio. Still, this ratio is a far cry from the (20:1) ratio we often see with today's digital bunch.

The dozens of takes per set-up goes all of the way back to the very first consumer-grade video cameras that hit the market back in the seventies. Tape was cheap and if you didn't like what you got, you would shoot it again. Not much has changed today, except it's even easier to over-cover the crap out of scenes. If you don't like what you get, just format the card and start over. This is a bad habit to get into and becomes a crutch; a disease called "convenience of technology". Demanding less than perfection, straight out of the gate, is somehow substantiated by the "we'll just keep going till we get it right" syndrome. Again, perfect planning along with plenty of rehearsal time is not just for the big boys in Hollywood. A (4:1) to (10:1) should still be a target ratio for the digital crowd as well.

The Coverage Factor

There are those directors who really like to get their fair share of coverage; however, too much of a good thing can soon turn ugly. It takes time to move the camera, move lighting instruments, reset the background props, and whatever else may be required for a given scene. As I mentioned before, it's the time between the takes that usually takes the most time.

Several years ago, I was hired as the gaffer for one of those miracle story TV shows. The show was designed as a "four story per segment" episodic reenactment show. This particular story or segment I was hired to work on had been shot up on Mt. Hood in Oregon. The story depicted a married couple whose car had gotten stranded in the snow at night. They made the decision to leave their car and take off on foot to find help. Lost and freezing with no idea of where they were, the miracle had them being rescued by a pack of wolves. Rather than eating the wayward drifters, the wolves offered hot chocolate and led them to a pay phone.

The amount of coverage the director demanded was beyond sufficient. Keep in mind, as I mentioned in the "Logistics" chapter, geography and season will play a huge part in how many hours per day or night one can be expected to film. Evidently this director knew full well that nighttime here in the Pacific Northwest, during winter, meant fifteen hours of darkness. He needed every minute of that darkness for the many set-ups he had planned. Along with a huge unnecessary company move, he required more coverage than would be needed for a DIY video on aircraft construction. We counted some ninety set-ups all packed into one night of principal photography. When aired, the shots that made the cut were less that one-tenth of what was captured.

Granted, there are scenes that require an abundance of coverage i.e. the car chase example earlier. Conversely, there are also scenes that don't warrant much coverage at all. What determines how much coverage a scene may require? Even though subjective, it often comes down to the director's confidence, knowledge and personality, especially if there are no storyboards. In other words, how apt is he or she when telling a story visually, without turning the thing into a fifteen thousand-piece jigsaw puzzle?

First up, we must clarify what we're referring to in terms of coverage. Coverage is everything the camera records using a multitude of compositions, angles and lenses. In other words, any and all establishing shots, close-ups, reversals and any other detail shots that may be desired. While it is true that some Director/DP teams can shoot enough coverage to assemble an entire alternate movie, there are those that don't get enough coverage for one. They ultimately leave the editor nothing to work with during the assembly process of story telling.

Take the earlier bank robber car chase scene as an example. How much coverage does it take to tell the story? Again, the amount of coverage for that scene is really dependent on how much money is available. We would hope enough to tell the story in a way that engages the audience. If we have Detective Barrett chasing off after the bank robbers in one shot, only to cut to him in the mall parking lot with the thieves standing there in handcuffs in the next shot, there'll be some very important story telling stuff missing. Scenes like that are going to require a bit more coverage if they're going to have any entertainment value.

In contrast, to request twenty-five different detail shots for something as simple as an actor sitting down at a kitchen table is a bit obsessive-compulsive. Five angles on just the chair being pulled away from the table, a close-up of the hand pulling the chair out, a close-up of the actor swinging his butt into the chair, a close-up of the chair's legs sliding on the floor back towards the table, and so on. This scenario, as ridiculous as it sounds, happens more often than not. The question comes down to, what are we trying to "sell" to the viewer? And, is there enough coverage for the editor to piece together a convincing tell of the story? This is where the rubber meets the road, so to speak. If an obscene amount of coverage is taken just for the sake of covering one's butt, then that's an issue that has more to do with the lack of a game plan i.e. storyboards, and a lack of experience on the part of the director.

Remember discipline? The simple fact is 35mm film is too expensive to frivolously experiment with haphazard set-ups. Even though not limited to 35 mm film, this same type of discipline should also be the directive of the digital indie filmmaker as well.

A friend of mine, who occasionally works as an extra for major films, was cast as a stand-in for an episodic pilot TV show. Principal photography lasted for five days and nights and rarely exceeded a twelve-hour day. The pilot was shot using a digital camera, not a film camera, yet they had the same disciplines of a film production. Granted, episodic TV demands moving along through principal photography at record pace; however, every shot and every detail was orchestrated and pre-planned as though it were brain surgery. Whether it was shot lists or storyboards they followed, they never deviated off course. They got exactly what was needed and then they moved on.

Storyboards and Shot Lists

As I've expressed in detail, the over coverage of any scene will eat the heck out of a production day faster than a monkey can eat a cupcake. The "guess what we're going to shoot" approach to filmmaking does nothing but expose incompetence.

Directors and DPs who are disciplined will follow storyboards as though they are roadmaps to a pile of money. This roadmap to success also pertains to the keys and everyone else on the project. It is the schematic, the big plan that keeps the production on task. Nothing will kill the day faster than a bunch of creative types inventing shots as they go. Storyboards are as much a part of the scheduling process as lights are as much a part of the filming process. Major productions use storyboards because they work.

Storyboards, or at the very least, a shot list for each and every scene, informs the cast and crew as to what's been completed and what's yet to complete. Not only does it save time, money and nerves, this practice also prevents the bad practice of making up shots on the fly. Some directors, along with some DPs, can easily get distracted by creativity. This isn't a bad thing, but unleashed, it can be serious reason for calamity when it comes to making the day's scheduled goal.

A Director/DP team I worked with some years ago, would occasionally take a little walk through the magic kingdom between set-ups, if you know what I mean. When they returned to the set, many new and interesting ideas would, all of a sudden, come into play. FYI, the magic kingdom approach to film making will make for a lot of extra work. We were, many times, forced to re-shoot scenes the way they had originally been planned, after the magic fog had cleared.

Just like with anything worthwhile, a plan must be made and then followed as closely as possible. To deviate from said plan occasionally is one thing, but to dismiss it altogether just for the sake of experiment is a plan that will inevitably cost more money.

The Company Move

There are many who believe that those of us who work in the motion picture industry have glamorous jobs. I've often said the only time this industry is glamorous is when speaking with those who are not in the biz. Working in the no/low budget independent film industry is a lot of hard work accompanied by long hours and crappy food. That being said, the last thing anyone wants to see on the call sheet is a company move.

Company moves happen for a myriad of reasons. They may be scheduled because of actor availability, location availability, weather, and/or a handful of other reasons. Whatever the reason, minimizing these laborious, time eating nuances can only be in a production's best interest.

Company moves will not go well when a plan does not include packing, loading and travel time. During one of the mornings of filming, I couldn't believe my eyes when I read the call sheet. There it was on the schedule; an 11:00 AM company move across town. This would put us on the 8th floor of a downtown office complex, miles from where the day would begin. On this particular day, they had scheduled the filming to begin at 11:30 AM. This meant we had to tear down, pack up, drive across town, park, unload, stage, get everything set up and be ready for the first shot all in a thirty minute time limit. Company moves do happen, it's the nature of the beast, and often they end up being a big pain regardless of how well they are executed. Had they included all of the other important factors pertaining to a company move, the day would not have become chaos on wheels.

We've spent some serious time on how important it is to be realistic with the schedule. Obviously the company move should be deserving of the same scheduling attention. A production must allow enough time to make everything happen. If the day begins at 6:00 AM and the company move to the next location is scheduled to begin at 11:00 AM, don't attempt to film detective Barrett's entire car chase scene prior to the big move. Scheduling long complex scenes prior to a company move never works.

It is common for the second location to be available for only a short period of time. For this reason, it is imperative that the production get to the location at exactly the scheduled time. The production must quickly get in, get the shot and quickly get out. Unfortunately, it's the shooting schedule prior to the company move that creates the biggest challenge. It's the over planning of set-ups and the amount of script pages required to get in the can prior to moving to the next location, that will throw a big monkey wrench into things. If at all possible, schedule company move days with lighter scenes and easier set-ups. In other words, don't plan scenes that would normally require a full day to shoot only to be crammed into a four-hour period before a move.

Watch for ridiculous unnecessary company moves. It may be much easier to turn the camera a few degrees and viola, a new location without ever leaving the farm. Of course this is something that should be ratified during the location/tech scout phase of the big enchilada. Going back a few pages to the Miracle TV show that was referenced, nature had provided us with plenty of snow since it was the dead of winter and we were at 9,000 feet elevation. And just in case, we also had special effects snow and wind machines helping Mother Nature. The lighting package wasn't all that big, but did sport a couple of 2500 watt HMIs among a few other choice lighting instruments. This meant the use of a generator, and all of its accessories, to help make-believe happen accordingly.

Other than where the picture car was located, stuck in the snow, there was virtually nothing but snow and trees for the other 350 degrees of camera view. The director made, what we all believed to be, a ridiculous unnecessary decision. He had us pack everything up and drive five or six miles to a new location. The new location was identical to the location we had just left, just no stranded car. Rather than turn the camera a few degrees left or right of said car, he thought it best for us to pack everything up and make the huge company move.

A big help in planning the company move day, if logistically possible, is to send a pre-rigging crew to the set in advance. This advanced forethought helps in relieving some of the stresses that are common with such moves. As long as the prior location doesn't require every light stand and flag the truck has available, sending some of that equipment and crew ahead earlier on, can be the difference between making the day or not. There'll be a more in-depth discussion on pre-rigging a little later on.

For us in the no/low budget world of movie making, there is always going to be the lack of bodies on the set to do the heavy labor. Just that alone should suggest one must plan accordingly. Company moves are a pain even for the big Hollywood productions. Maintaining the crew's sanity should be more than just a side thought, especially since they're not getting much pay. Their mental and physical states of well being are already stretched to the maximum day in and day out. It is the crew who contributes greatly to the success of a film. Working with them, not against them, can only help ensure a quality product. A good UPM will know when and how to best schedule the much-despised company move. As long as the schedule is followed as closely as possible, it shouldn't become a complete morale killer.

If you can't shoot it in ten hours, go back to film school

Chapter Six

SEQUENCING, CONTINUITY
and the
SCRIPT SUPERVISOR

Sequencing a Plan

When a script is to become a movie, shooting the story in the order in which it is written will probably not be a first consideration. In fact, movies are hardly ever shot in the order they're written. Filming a movie out of the sequence in which it was written, by design, saves time, money and labor, among many other important things. From the time the UPM gets the script, he or she will arrange the sequence of scenes in which the movie will be shot. Factors that influence the filming order have much to do with time of day or night, season, location, and actor availabilities, just to name a few.

Let's say, for example, we have a downtown bistro scene to film. Our characters are a husband and wife team that meets up for lunch. We'll refer to them as Monica and James. Monica exits her place of work, James pulls up via cab, they meet and greet in front of Monica's building, and then they walk around the corner and enter a small romantic bistro. They exchange dialogue, exit and go their separate ways.

Location availability is one factor that is, no doubt, at the top of the list when considering the sequence in which a scene is to be filmed. For the part of the scene that takes place inside the bistro, let's assume there are six pages of dialogue. It is a very good possibility that the interior portion of the bistro scene altogether could take a couple of days to shoot, if not planned properly. Remember, we're the no/low budget bunch, so closing the bistro for a couple of consecutive days is probably out of the question. Filming the interior of the bistro will require breaking down and sequencing the scene in order to fit everything into one day. The one main factor that will influence the sequencing of the interior of the bistro scene hinges on the time of day the story takes place. There will be more on this subject matter a little later.

Actor availability is also a concern when trying to establish a sequential shooting schedule. Actors who sign on for the no/low budget type films usually have day jobs, or at least they should, that is if they want to eat. Because of their employment and other scheduling issues, it will be necessary at some point or another to accommodate them. Unfortunately, this is where things can cause much frustration. Everyone is available except for one. Then when that one is available, there's someone else who is not available. Filming out of sequence and dancing from location to location may be the only way to keep from wasting the day.

Have you ever wondered what happens when a prominent actor dies mid-production, yet the movie still gets completed? It's not often that the production company is able to hire a look-alike to replace the dead actor's character, that is if they're required to speak. The sequence in which a movie is shot is the big insurance policy that productions many times rely upon.

While the number of actors who decide to leap to their demise from a ten-story building right in the middle of production is few, they do have a tendency to quit every now and then. That is, of course, if they're working with us, the no/low budget bunch. Other than an over-dose, this is the most likely reason a lead actor will be leaving our project mid-way through. But what if he or she does leave, now what? I can hear the emergency production meeting that night in the motor home, "Have we finished all the scenes this rube is supposed to be in?" If not, "What do we do now?" This is where sequencing could have saved the day.

Depending on the script, it may be possible to shoot all of the flakey character's scenes during one specified block of time. This will at least guarantee that person's part, in its entirety, is in the can. It would behoove the production to shoot those scenes first if there is any chance he or she may leave the project early. If, however, that person's part is continuous throughout the story and he or she leaves mid-stream, the production could be screwed.

There are times when a no/low budget film is in a position to hire a ringer for a particular role. A ringer is an actor that is considered to be a "B-list" personality, one who has a minor box office name. Unless the ringer has just been released from rehab or prison, he or she is probably not going to be hanging around the set for any length of time. This would suggest flying them in, filming their scene or scenes and then flying them back to from whence they came. That said, every scene the so-called star is required to be in, had best be in the can.

Last but not least, the order in which a film is shot must also consider the season the story has chosen as its backdrop. For example, if the story involves a season such as autumn, that season then becomes a character within the story. All exterior scenes will require an autumn appearance such as reddish, yellow leaves on trees as well as on the ground. If it's a winter setting, then snow may be the backdrop. This will also be a factor when filming interiors, as the camera may expose the exterior through any windows or open doors. I know this has more to do with the subject of continuity, but it's certainly relevant when considering the sequence in which a film is shot. For most no/low budget films, they're usually filmed within a thirty-day principal photography time frame. That being said, one would assume a season would easily be in play for at least that length of time; however, that is only true as long there are no exterior pick-up scenes that aren't realized until the next season, just a thought.

Whether actor availability, locations or seasonal issues, the sequence in which a film is shot will play a big role in stress, scheduling and expense. This raises another briefly touched on issue and that is continuity.

At the beginning of the "Under the Walnut Tree" production, we had an actress who stipulated that because of her character's extreme demands, she requested the movie be shot in sequence. For whatever reason, the hierarchy agreed to her demand. The beginning of the story portrayed our lead actress hooked on crack, heroin, cocaine, and of course anything else she could get her hands on. In other words, her character was that of an urban bred, white trash, crack whore. The end of the story depicted her character months after rehabilitation. The big issue no one saw coming was that she had lost thirty-plus pounds during the two months of filming. Had we shot the beginning of the movie last, she would have truly looked the part; however, because of her weight loss throughout the production, just the opposite happened. Because of the sequence in which the film was edited together, she appeared gaunt and unhealthy at the end of the story, at the time she should have been appearing healthy and of average weight. Here's the rub, because the movie was shot sequentially, at least at the beginning, any pick-up scenes required from the beginning of the schedule, should have been filmed within days of the original filming of those scenes. The shooting in sequence approach ultimately created a huge continuity snafu. So here we were with a pick-up scene that needed to tie together with the master scene, which was shot a month-and-a-half prior. In the scene, our gaunt, undernourished crack whore exits her boyfriend's car weighing a whopping one- hundred pounds soaking wet. (The pick-up shot, day forty-five of the production). She is next seen entering her apartment thirty pounds heavier. (Day two of the production) Maybe no one will notice...

Sequencing and continuity are major issues for any motion picture. Other than bad directing, bad writing and bad acting, the issues of sequencing and continuity will doom a film faster than red licorice disappears off of the craft service table.

The Physics of Meteorological Continuity

Maintaining a consistent appearance within the story is what separates the good from the bad. If ever there's a time to be vigilant about the task of minding continuity, it's when filming out of sequence, especially while dealing with Mother Nature at the same time.

This is where a basic understanding of natural physics, meteorology and the science of light is vital. To begin, let's consider weather and time of day for our first of many continuity concerns.

In the no/low budget filmmaking world, we are forced to deal with weather and time-related continuity situations with a much greater concern than that of the better funded Hollywood production. The fact that the no/low budget indie film simply doesn't have the big-boy toy resources to control the weather, time of day and light, means that we must always rely on being very inventive.

Take the before mentioned bistro scene with Monica and James. It would look weird to have our couple meet on the sidewalk during a torrential downpour only to have them entering the bistro just around the corner in bright sunlight. Consider the fact that there may be several days, if not weeks, between part one of a scene and part two of the same scene. That said, you can pretty much be assured the weather will change from one day to the next, blowing even a sliver of a chance of maintaining any aspect of meteorological continuity.

During the later days of the "Under the Walnut Tree" production, we found ourselves entering into the fall months and, of course, the weather wasn't cooperating. It was a constant battle scheduling days that wouldn't be raining. It never failed. Towards the end of principal photography, the days were either raining or about to rain. What started out in the beginning as warm and sunny quickly became cold, grey and wet. Unfortunately, there wasn't much that could be done but wait for breaks in the weather.

Up here in the Pacific Northwest where a majority of my work is performed, it is almost impossible to determine what the weather will be from day to day, let alone six or seven days down the road. For this reason, having some kind of weather related back-up plan is a must.

Not exactly related to weather, but time of day or night in which the story is to take place, is also of great concern. Could the entire bistro scene be filmed in sequence from beginning to end all in one afternoon? No. The bistro scene is way too long. Any continuity would be non-existent and, no doubt, fly out of the very bistro window we'd be attempting to shoot. The lighting, in conjunction with time of day, would change drastically, all in a matter of seconds, as viewed from the audience. If indeed shot sequentially, by the time our couple actually exited the bistro, it would probably be nighttime. Breaking down the bistro scene into many sub scenes would clarify time and space for the audience by maintaining that ever-important continuity factor.

In relation to the story, Monica and James are sitting in the bistro for maybe thirty minutes or so during their perceived lunch hour setting. To maintain continuity for the viewer, the entrance and exit to the bistro must be shot around the same time of day; at least within a couple of hours of make-believe movie time. If they are to enter at lunch time and exit at the end of lunch time, it would be necessary to mimic the lunch hour look in both weather and lighting for the audience to believe the story. If this sounds like a big "duh" factor, I promise it's simple details like these that can be the easiest to overlook.

One particular scene during the filming of "Under the Walnut Tree" comes to mind. We had just completed the lighting for a scene that had our lead character walking up to a grave at night. The call for the camera to roll is heard, followed by "Action". Our lead character walks up to her mark and begins delivering her lines when the director immediately interrupts, calling out "Cut". The director had, at that time, realized there was a continuity issue. Because the scene was shot out of sequence, the beginning part of that scene was shot several days prior. No one, including the script supervisor, thought to check the time of day in story time, when that whole scene was to take place. It was a good thing the director caught this little oversight. If not, the finished edit would have had our actress walking from her first position during daylight, only to have her land on her second position, fifteen feet away, at night.

There must always be detailed documentation for each and every set-up and scene. This is most important when working on exterior day sets. These notes should include season, time of day, sun track and position, weather conditions, sky color (cloud cover or not) lens compass heading and ambient f-stop. Along with what lighting instruments are used, they should also include what, if any, color correction is applied, what color temperature the camera is set to, and what, if any, filters are utilized. If there is ever a reason to return to a particular location for a pick-up scene, and there will be, make dang sure all of the necessary specifics are well documented to maintain atmospheric continuity.

New World Scenes

Some time ago I came up with the term "New World". It's a term used to reference a scene that has no lighting or weather connection to any other context within the movie. For example:

Consider the bistro scene: EXTERIOR - DAY - RAIN Monica exits her downtown place of business to meet with James for lunch. James exits his cab in front of Monica's building, just as Monica exits and they meet, greet and kiss. Together they walk down the sidewalk and enter the local bistro just around the corner. INTERIOR - DAY - RAIN the scene continues inside the bistro and they have their dialogue and then get up to exit. EXTERIOR - DAY - RAIN they exit the bistro, then each go their separate ways, end of scene.

From the DP and gaffer's point of view, this scene takes place in a new time in space. This scene, in its entirety has no connection to any other scene or scenes within the movie with regards to time of day, lighting and weather. It's a stand-alone scene, which would be considered a "New World" scene.

We do need, however, to take this scenario a bit further. During the filming process, the bistro scene will be broken into small individual scene elements and we will need to consider maintaining lighting and atmospheric consistencies for the entire scene as a whole. If you look at it like this, whenever the camera moves, it would be considered another small scene or set-up. The meet and greet on the sidewalk is a small scene within the whole bistro scene of which there'll be multiple set-ups. There are the camera angles that portray our couple walking to the bistro, which again require multiple set-ups; another scene. Our couple would need to be filmed entering and exiting the bistro from the exterior point of view, which would be two more scenes. And, last but not least, the interior of the bistro would be yet another scene with all of its associated set-ups, all of which suggests it should be daylight and raining for each and every one of the many set-ups.

It's the set-ups within a scene that take the scene breakdown process even further. Every time the camera changes position or lenses, those changes equate to a different set-up. If you've ever seen a slate (clapper board) you'll notice that the scene numbers are many times followed by letters, i.e. (Scene 43A, B, C, etc.). Those letters define a change in camera angle, position, or lenses within that scene. If for example the bistro scene as a whole is referred to as scene "43", it's possible that by the time the bistro is finished, the many set-ups could take scene 43 and add to that a corresponding letter, possibly going through the alphabet one, two or even three times. (Scene "43RRR") The meticulous breaking apart of scenes by camera placement, framing and lens choice is not only designed for interesting story telling purposes, but it's very important to the editor. The editing together of the film so it makes sense to the audience is the editor's main claim to fame. It is his or her job to assemble all of the footage and tell a story that best captivates the audience. It makes sense then that the editor would need to have elements such as lighting and weather match within a particular scene to ensure continuity throughout.

Continuity and Interior Scenes

As we've learned so far, there is much to consider when dealing with natural light and atmospheric conditions since they are the two forces of nature we have little control over. Therefore we should take into consideration every possible scenario Mother Nature can throw at us, even when working with an interior set which is on location. For us filmmakers, there are only two stages on which we work, the interior stage and the exterior stage. Of course, those two stages can be broken down even further, interior night, interior day and exterior night, exterior day.

To help understand how we arrive at the two stages, and how atmospheric continuity plays an intrical part in the telling of the story, let's see how our bistro scene would look as a Broadway play.

A theatrical performance or play has but one stage on which all scenes take place. The stage is that big raised platform in front of all of the seats. Just making sure we're all on the same page here. For the Broadway production of the bistro scene, the set builders would be required to construct two separate stage settings or sets. These would include the exterior set, which would consist of the street, sidewalk and downtown buildings to mimic the look of outdoors. Then there would be the construction of the interior set, i.e. the interior of the bistro. Either one of the two sets (interior or exterior) would be rolled into place on a specified cue, separated by a curtain closing and reopening process. The rain effects for the exterior setting would be controlled from the lighting and effects control booth.

For our film version of the same scenario, it's the editing process that divides the two interior/exterior stage settings, instead of the curtain. Unlike working on a Broadway stage with its consistent lighting and on and off rain cues, a film location will always be subject to inclement weather conditions. There are always going to be atmospheric and lighting conditions that must be dealt with every minute of the day for the real-world stage. It's those same exterior conditions though that can also influence the interior look as the camera sees them. The good news is that the filming of an interior on-location set can be scheduled to accommodate such issues more easily, even when windows and doors are considered.

For DP/Gaffer considerations, we would have composed our shot from just inside the door for Monica and James's entrance and exit. Since the scene in the story is established as a rainy day, Monica and James must, at the very least, make their entrance in wet clothing along with wet hair. The exterior lighting and weather, if viewed from the camera's angle inside looking out must match what was filmed or going to be filmed, from the exterior point of view. Obviously for us no/low budget bunch, it would be smart for us to shoot that scene when Mother Nature is scheduled to do her thing, as in rain. If not, it's the ol' garden hose and spray-nozzle routine or cheat the action to take place at a camera position that doesn't expose the exterior. ("Cheating" is a term used within the industry that refers to the positioning of the camera or actors one direction or another in order to obtain a different perspective.) Monica and James's exit from the bistro should be shot at the same time as their entrance, since the camera is already in a relative position. However for their exit, we would not want Monica and James appearing wet, as they would have dried out a bit before exiting the bistro.

If our bistro scene has our couple sitting at a table next to a window, the shot would, no doubt, expose whatever outdoor weather and lighting conditions are present at the time. This means that the weather and lighting conditions that were part of the exterior portion of the bistro scene had best match the interior scenes as well.

There are but only four choices. Schedule the filming to take place when it's actually raining. Add special effects rain to the exterior. Move James and Monica away from any visible windows. Or, fix it in post. The latter is really not an option.

Hopefully there has been a concise, well thought out plan of attack that addresses such issues. Placing our two characters away from any visible windows would obviously be the cheapest solution. Nevertheless, interiors are easy to shoot compared to battling the many atmospheric factors associated with exterior locations.

Continuity and Exterior Scenes

Let's take a look at a quick summary of our bistro scene again. It takes place with Monica exiting her place of employment in downtown Filmville. James enters the scene by way of cab directly in front of her building. They meet on the sidewalk, and together they quickly walk in the rain, around the corner, and enter the bistro for lunch. After their lunch and dialogue they exit the bistro and go their separate ways. Let's also assume we've already shot all of the interior bistro scenes several days prior. And last but not least, to help minimize special effects costs, we've chosen an actual rainy day for the filming of said exteriors. Filming here in the Pacific Northwest, we can be relatively sure it will be raining that day anyway. The bistro scene, in its entirety, will be "New World" so matching any elements of the bistro scene to any other part of the movie will not be a concern.

Geographic locations and their predominating weather patterns should always be a factor when planning any indie film production. If a particular film location has weather patterns that are mostly sunny year round, choosing a rain-ridden backdrop is going to be expensive to produce. For the no/low budget film production, choosing the normal average weather pattern for the backdrop is certainly the easier, cheaper way to go. For our application, shooting the bistro scene in Seattle, even if the rain does stop which is unlikely, small rain gags would be implemented to enhance the shot regardless.

Using rain as a character can certainly set a tone or feeling for a particular scene. We've all seen the movie where black-suited extras sporting black umbrellas stand around the proverbial grave as torrents of rain fall. For this, the rain character is used to sell sadness. A grey rainy day is a popular backdrop for a funeral scene. Or it's the rain, wind and lightning that sells fear to the audience, as the sexy seductress navigates her way through the old, spooky house during a suspense filled horror film. For our story, we're going to use rain to sell the location of our story, which is Seattle.

Not only will the rainy day setting say something about the location in which our story takes place, it will also allow us to be more flexible as to how to approach the day's required shots. In other words, for us no/low budget bunch, shooting on a rainy day will actually help save us time and money.

Establishing "Establishing Shots"

As we arrive on location, the first order of business is to set up for an establishing shot or two. The establishing shots will sell the setting, i.e. locale, time of day and weather. This is where experience will determine the success of the day. There does not need to be a hundred different angles for establishing shots. Ask the question, will the shot or shots make or break the film? Too many unnecessary establishing shots will take its toll on the schedule. I have worked with directors who require one or two masters to establish a setting, and I have worked with directors who begin their coverage from the International Space Station and work their way in from there. I've mentioned this before, but it deserves repeating. Having storyboards and following them will guarantee the correct amount of shots for the story.

Let's get back to our arrival at the location and let's assume rain is falling. This would be a great time to quickly prep and set-up for those much-needed establishing shots. We will choose a wide lens to capture the locale along with the action of our characters. Here's a time-saver trick; with the action being far in the distance, critical hair and make-up need not be a concern. In fact, look-a-likes dressed the same could easily be used while our lead actors are in make-up.

All equipment, crew and anything that does not belong in the shot would obviously need to be clear of the camera's frame. This will require an out-of-the-way staging area for grip and lighting equipment, possibly inside the building Monica exits from. From the rooftop across the street, the first establishing shot of Monica exiting her place of employment as James pulls up in the cab is captured. They perform their meet and greet, walk down the sidewalk and continue around the corner.

We'll also want a wide shot or two of Monica and James both entering and exiting the bistro. Easily and quickly performed, all of the wide establishing shots could easily be accomplished in the first two hours of the day. Unless our photo doubles are drunk, this shouldn't require but a couple of takes each. With those done and out of the way early, we can now move in for the close-ups with our key talent. "Someone go get our lead actors out of hair and makeup. We're ready for them."

More Rain, Please

Even though we've picked a day where the exterior bistro scene takes place in actual rain, additional special effects rain manufacturing equipment will still be required for continuity and added visual stimulation. Whether it's fire hoses connected to a giant rain bar hanging from a 20-ton crane or a garden hose with a spray nozzle, rain is a must. My guess is it's going to be the garden hose approach. The beauty of having all of the wide establishing shots out of the way during a natural rainstorm is that the close-ups will be easy as long as it at least remains mostly cloudy. As long as we have grey skies, the close-ups, and tracking and reversal shots can be accomplished using small, inexpensive rain gag equipment.

Here's a question I often get asked: Is it better to film in the rain or in direct sunlight? Again subjective, but for the no/low budget approach to something like the bistro scene, I'd be more inclined to film on a rainy day. However, for the "Under the Walnut Tree" production, during the time we were filming under the big walnut tree, rain or even clouds were out of the question. It would have been too dark under said tree for the amount of power and lights we had available.

For the bistro scene, let's assume we had chosen a sunny day as the backdrop for our couple's lunchtime rendezvous. It would have been the track of the sun throughout the day we would have had to contend with. The direction from whence the sunlight came throughout the day, and the shadows produced, would be the biggest of concerns. We would have had to plan specific times of the day to grab certain shots, not to mention additional lighting control devices available to use when needed. Remember, lighting continuity is always a huge concern.

The establishing wide shots we chose to get out of the way first thing in the morning for the "rainy day bistro scene" could not have taken place at that time if it were sunny. There is an old saying, "Only fools and beginners film at high noon." This saying is in reference to ugly facial shadow issues. Depending on latitudinal location and season, the sun is usually in a more overhead position during the noon hour, which will create some pretty ugly shadows on the face. To help nullify these atrocities, close-up shots should take place either in the early morning or in the late afternoon when the sun is low in the horizon. This standard approach to filming in sunlight may satisfy aesthetic issues, but unless you're well prepared, there still will be more than a fare share of continuity issues to contend with.

Even though the sun will be low in the sky when filming during the morning hours, the sun still continues to rise. This means shadows on the face will change as the sun rises. This will affect lighting continuity unless some drastic lighting measures are taken. Shooting on a sunny day is fine as long as there are tools of the trade to solve such issues. This includes big lighting instruments and lots of overheads (silks, nets and solids).

In summary, again using the bistro scene as the example, the wide establishing could be accomplished any time of day as long as it was raining. All close-up shots could also be accomplished any time of day as long as it was at least cloudy. On a sunny day, there wouldn't be that kind of latitude. All close-up shots would have to be accomplished early in the morning or late in the afternoon, during the pretty-lighting time of day. All wide establishing shots would need to be accomplished when the sun is at its highest position, the ugly-lighting time of day.

As mentioned in chapter three "Logistics of the Sun", the compass direction of buildings and sidewalks in relation to the track of the sun must also be taken into consideration. Choosing buildings and sidewalks that run east and west may be necessary to best accommodate the track of the sun. For the bistro scene, having buildings that face north and/or south will allow us to film our couple's close-ups early in the morning or late in the afternoon, while the sun is low in the sky.

This would suggest that the bistro's entrance should also face north and/or south. That being said, the bistro's actual location can't really be around the corner, as the audience would be led to believe. We would still need our low sun to work with us for all of the close-ups for the entrance and exit scenes of the bistro as well.

Sunlight is a normal exterior lighting situation. It just requires a different approach to control. When dealing with the sun and no/low budget, it is possible that more days will need to be scheduled in order to shoot exterior scenes as exampled in the bistro scene. Of course, that would depend on the amount of coverage and the number of takes. Obviously, if there is the lighting control equipment wherewithal to accomplish the scene in direct sunlight, go for it. However, for the no/low budget renegades, the cloudy rainy day is by far the cheaper way to go.

Atmospheric and lighting continuity is only part of the many concerns for the matching of scenes and set-ups. Wardrobe, property and props also have to match from set-up to set-up and scene to scene.

The Script Supervisor

Let's assume the scene that leads into the bistro scene has Monica and James dressing for work in their small downtown apartment. It's obvious they'd be getting dressed into the wardrobe they would be wearing for their lunchtime rendezvous later. Otherwise, there'd have to be some explanation as to why either or both of them are dressed in different clothing seconds later in the bistro. Keep in mind that while the passage of make-believe time on-screen may only be a few seconds apart, the filming of the scenes may actually take place days or even weeks apart. This gap in time between filming the two scenes can easily be the end of continuity as we know it, if not careful.

We've all witnessed the arbitrary scene that depicts the guy holding a bottle of booze in his right hand (camera angle "A") and in the next set-up (camera angle "B") he's holding a glass of booze, but this time it's in his left hand. A good script supervisor will take massive amounts of notes detailing every piece of wardrobe, hairdo, make-up and prop on the set. The length of a cigar is duly noted, photographed and tagged. A "hot-set" implies nothing is to be touched or, heaven forbid, moved in any way shape or fashion before, during and after filming, at least until the set is wrapped for good. Whether it's a prop, set piece, ding, dent, chip or splatter, everything in front of the lens must be meticulously noted. It's not a matter of "if" it's going to be seen again, it's "when" it's going to be seen again. And, will it always look the same?

I just met with the director for the "Under the Walnut Tree" production the other day. With principal photography long behind us, the postproduction team is, for the most part, knee deep into the editing process. As we began talking about the production and its progress, the director's anger and frustration suddenly erupted when the subject of continuity came up. The multitude of continuity issues they had to constantly deal with were enough to send him over the edge. It was obvious the script supervisor was not competent at doing her job.

The script supervisor's job is not one that should be taken lightly. It takes someone who has an inherent propensity for paying attention to details. Just like with any of the other key positions, a script supervisor who really knows his or her craft is worth his or her weight in gold.

Wardrobe/Property

There is no bigger waste of time than having to wait for an actor to retrieve even one small piece of wardrobe or prop from his or her trailer, hotel, car or even home. Any wardrobe/property master who allows an actor to take their wardrobe and/or prop accessories home should be immediately fired, and never allowed back on the set. There is absolutely no excuse for an actor to take away from the set anything that is a part of the production. If it were up to me, actors would arrive naked and depart naked. I cannot begin to tell you how many times this has been an issue while working on certain less-disciplined productions.

At the very least, get a wardrobe and property van or truck that is always a part of the production caravan. Where the production goes, the wardrobe-prop truck goes. Hire someone who is solely responsible for the wardrobe and props. Their job is to secure, maintain, transport, bag, tag and supply wardrobe, gloves, guns, knives, bottles, glasses, dishes, rags and every other non-breathing entity that plays a part in the film. When the camera is ready to roll, property and wardrobe, including all accessories, should be ready to go as well.

The Art Department/Production Designer

For the super no/low budget bunch, there's probably not much hope in hiring a real honest-to-goodness Hollywood production designer and a battalion of art department pros. When talking with those who are in the production designing/art department positions, their eyes light up when they describe their job. For these individuals this a position that is as fun and creative as it gets. They love what they do and what they bring to the look of a film. If you take a moment to truly understand what's involved in the set design position, you can't help but be amazed at the incredible magic they perform.

For those who aren't totally savvy to the production designer/art department positions, allow me to expand a bit. These individuals are a breed unto themselves. They know history like nobody's business. Any period of time or setting that's required for story telling purposes, they've got it handled. A movie or scene that's set in a different time period than the present is commonly referred to as a "period piece". For example, if a story requires a 1940's era backdrop, everything in front of the lens will be 1940's stuff, thanks to the design/art department team, and that means everything; houses, cars, buildings, signage, props and wardrobe, and even era color and paint schemes. The production design team designs and builds sets, and works with the art department in designing and providing the look for interior and exterior set pieces, furnishings and props. The main reason the no/low budget independent film uses the modern day backdrop is that there simply isn't the money for cool, believable looking time travel.

That means the no/low budget production designer/art department person must work that much harder to make magic happen. He or she needs to know where and how to get all of the furnishings, set pieces and props that are required. He or she will also need to have them on the set, in place and ready. This is no easy task when working with a very thin budget. It's where a little help from everyone on the production may save the day.

For the no/low budget production designer/art department position, finding someone who's artistically minded is an obvious plus; however, someone who communicates his or her needs well is even better. Some time ago I was working on a film when, on the scheduled day of the shoot, the art department dude was screaming on his cell phone, desperately looking for a Harley Davidson motorcycle to be used as a background element for a particular scene. Of course his demands were coming at the very last minute. Had he asked around a few days prior, he would have known well in advance that two of us on the set owned such motorcycles. I would have easily brought mine had I known. The old adage, "Look for the diamonds in your own back yard first," is probably one of the smartest rules to follow, at this point. Not once, but dozens of times, I've heard the grumblings from those who rule over property, wishing they had a specific item available on the day of the shoot. It takes no time at all to pass around a list of "prop-wants" during the pre-production process. If everyone, including producers and PAs get said list, chances are some items can be secured without ever leaving the farm.

Cleaning Supplies

We had just finished rigging a car for a driving shot. During the process, the windshield of the vehicle got smudged with fingerprints. I asked for glass cleaner and paper towels so I could clean up my mess. You would have thought I'd asked for plutonium 235. No one had thought to bring any cleaning supplies. Cleaning supplies on the set are as important as an oxygen tank is for a 95-year-old pneumonia patient. There again was time wasted looking for a bottle of glass cleaner and two lousy sheets of paper towels. The art department should, at the very least, provide glass cleaner and paper towels. Preferably an assortment of rags, bar towels, and bath towels should also be on the list of must haves. It never fails. Something will get spilled, smudged or dirty. Being prepared for such calamities should be a big "Duh".

To make sense out of nonsense makes sense.

Chapter Seven

PRODUCTION VALUE

A great story, superb acting, and awesome locations along with high-end production value are any director's dream. However, in the no/low budget world, just finding actors that can hit their marks while delivering their lines can be more than a small challenge. That being said, it is a foregone conclusion that having any degree of production value may be the only saving grace for the no/low budget film. So what adds to the production value? Yes, it starts with a great story complemented by great performances; however, there is so much more that can contribute to the value of a production. While grandiose special effects, car chases and elaborate sets are great, they also come with hefty price tags. There is, however, the less obvious production value additives such as, creative lighting designs, cool camera work and a dash of atmospheric effects here and there.

The Value of Lighting

Today, cameras are getting smaller, lighter and more compact than ever, all the while delivering great cinematic images that are absolutely out of this world. Recently, I was watching a TV commercial sensationalizing a popular SLR 35mm camera that was sporting the cine 24 fps feature.

The footage was amazing; however, it didn't take a Houdini to reveal their little trick. The great looks they were getting had more to do with their great lighting. Simply put, they had a nice budget that allowed for some awesome lighting. They could have used a twenty-dollar point-and-shoot and it would have looked great.

Not to get too far into the subject of lighting just yet, it is a fact that any film production must have lights. And taking that premise one step further, having a creative lighting design concept will only enhance the film that much more. In other words, having someone on board that understands lighting design and how to use lighting instruments is a must. Why this very important basic element of film school 101 seems to evade some no/low budget productions is beyond rational. I suspect it's the big budget SLR TV commercials that have conned the new-to-industry filmmaker into believing…"What you see is what you get."

The art of lighting is more than just illumination. If it were that easy, the DP would just flip on the house lights and film away. Movies, TV commercials and even industrial films are entered into with lighting design in mind. In other words, how is light going to influence the emotion of a scene? Accomplished DPs have created for themselves signatures for their lighting design.

Unfortunately, for the no/low budget filmmaker, it's the deficit of lighting instruments that can make this important artistic expression so frustrating and difficult. Having even the smallest of budgets, one should still consider how important lighting is to the telling of a story. Not only is light important for exposure and continuity, it's lighting that stimulates emotion. Many times, I refer to this as painting with light. There is a popular artist that refers to himself as the 'Painter of Light", but even by its own phraseological interpretation, a painter of light can be anyone who uses light for a creative medium. Understanding the science of how light works and what lighting instruments do what, is an absolute must for this industry. With a little knowledge, even the smallest of lighting packages can be made to look epic.

While having six semi trailers packed to the ceiling with grip and lighting is a DP's dream come true, it's not always the size of the package that makes for great lighting. There is much that can be done with little. It is obviously more frustrating, but it can be done. If DPing is your life's ambition but you lack the wherewithal to truly make your project look great, hire a good Assistant Cameraman; they'll help with understanding the ins and outs of the camera. Also, hire an experienced Gaffer; they'll have the chops to help paint the scenes so they look amazing. Remember, it's all about production value.

Later I will get into the subject of lighting in greater detail. But for now, just understand that lighting and the creative approach to painting scenes with said light is, and will be, directly proportionate to perceived production value.

It is important for the new-to-industry novice DP to learn the basics of lighting. Without an understanding of the rules, how would one know when the rules can be broken?

Motion Picture versus Camera Motion

Back in the early eighties when consumer grade video cameras first began flooding the market, the average beginner DP/camera operator used the zoom control toggle as though he or she were milking a cow. The over-use of the zoom control, fast pans to the left and the right would make anyone who saw the footage sick to their stomachs. Conversely there were those that were afraid to move the camera at all, as if it were cemented to a two-ton rock. It was a time where trial and error was the process by which we learned. Back in those days there weren't many inexpensive camera motion devises available for the indie no/low budget bunch. We found ourselves having to improvise almost every creative shot we wanted.

Those of us inventive types would use grocery carts, wheelchairs, bicycles and skateboards and anything else we could get our hands on to get the cool shots and we still do today. If it were crane shots we wanted, we made teeter-totter type devices out of ten-foot two-by-fours, a saw horse and rope. It wasn't until Jim Stanton invented the Jimmy Jib that we indeed had something remotely professional to work with. Today there's a cornucopia of indie-film camera motion toys that add much to the production value if used.

Having enough flexibility in the budget to rent or purchase a few camera movement accessories will certainly do wonders. For those that believe garage tinkering something into fashion will save money, think again. Unless extremely gifted or schooled in engineering, very seldom does building out of scrap, camera motion equipment, work.

A long-time DP friend of mine is what one would consider a shade-tree inventor. We often refer to him as the mad professor. His shop looks like the after effects of an explosion at a nuts and bolts factory. Always trying to reinvent the wheel, the guy has constructed more camera motion devices than Ronco has Kitchen Magicians. Out of everything he has built, I can only think of a couple of items that actually worked as intended. Industry standard equipment designed and manufactured by professional engineers, while expensive, does indeed work as intended. Their research and development departments spend thousands of man-hours and money developing products that are tried, true and tested to do exactly what they are designed to do. Personally, I believe spending time to raise the money to purchase or rent professionally manufactured, industry-standard equipment is time and money better spent.

The "Under the Walnut Tree" production had made the decision to build a dolly. The finished product was made of a three-foot by four-foot piece of plywood with skateboard wheels mounted to the underside. The idea was to roll the makeshift dolly along a couple of ten-foot lengths of PVC pipe. Not a terribly bad idea had the ground been level. However, we were under the walnut tree and the terrain was so uneven the dolly move was more of a carnival ride, lots of fun but totally useless. The question comes to mind; what would it have cost to have on the truck a doorway dolly, speed wheels and three or four lengths of industry standard dolly track to use as needed? That alone would have added tons to the production value. In their defense, they did utilize a small manual portable Jib, which did help add some to the production value.

Dolly versus Steadicam

Talking with a DP friend of mind, he reminded me of a big Hollywood movie production from some time ago and how they were able to save the day and the budget at the last minute. The production was up against the clock and dolly shots were proving to be too time-consuming. Not wanting to jeopardize production value, they had made the decision to incorporate a Steadicam. During the DVD interview, the director had stated that had they continued using the dolly/track system for the remainder of the shoot, they would have never made the schedule and would have gone over budget. If ever you've had the opportunity to work with a Fisher Ten dolly with its associated hardware and track, you are aware of the cost in time for such a shot. Even working with a doorway dolly, speed wheels and couple lengths of track can take a considerable amount of time to set up.

If there's a budget for track and dolly, there's probably the budget for a Steadicam. The time saved by not having to set up and level six lengths of dolly track may easily pay for a Steadicam, thereby moving the production along at a much faster pace. Here's the rub, there must also be in the budget the wherewithal to hire a qualified Steadicam operator. The thought of bringing to the project a Steadicam in the hopes that someone on the crew can strap the thing on and go for it is beyond ludicrous. Steadicams take years to master. There is though, another option. With cameras getting smaller there are the smaller hand held type camera stabilizers available for us no/low budget bunch. And those I've worked with are quite a bit easier to master. The shots are fluid and usually work just fine under most conditions. A thin budget doesn't necessarily mean having to limit dolly shots to grocery carts and wheelchairs.

Shortly after 9/11, a good friend of mine, who's a Director/ Cameraman, and I were contracted to film what was then titled the "Driving America" campaign. This was a yearlong gig for us, shooting a multitude of TV commercials for a large auto dealer franchise throughout several Midwest and Western states. The ad agency that hired us had used us many times before and was already very familiar with our work. We both wore many hats, which made us a two-man team for the most part. Ed owned the Jimmy Jib III, and was the Director/Cameraman, (the Director and Director of Photography in commercial terms). I was the crane operator and gaffer. Not to sound over boastful but, together we created some pretty amazing imagery. Obviously packing around twenty plus flight cases from airport to airport had its challenges, especially after 9/11, but what a blast.

One shot in particular that comes to mind took place on a gravel farming road thirty or forty miles outside of Omaha, Nebraska. We set up our shot along side the road very early in the morning. Just as the sun came up, the shot had our hero car traveling north, toward us at about thirty miles per hour. The car came up over the hill and down the other side directly toward the camera that was mounted to the end of the eighteen foot Jimmy Jib resting in the middle of the road. We timed the shot so the camera would rise up from the ground just feet before the front of the approaching car. The camera would rise and the car would pass under. The camera boom would, at the same time, swing to the right and we would simultaneously pan the camera to the left exposing the backlit golden fields of wheat. It was a million dollar shot. The jib made for spectacular creative imagery throughout the entire campaign, adding tons to the overall production value.

Camera motion equipment such as jibs, dollies or camera stabilizers, should rank high on the "must-have" list. For the no/low budget independent film, a little camera motion can go a long way.

The Bridging of Scenes

The cinematographer's ability to visually tell a story is as much of an art form as an artist's ability to tell his or her story in a painting. His or her talent goes way beyond just capturing the action; it's how they blend the action and or scenes together with other scenes that help the story breathe. The DP's approach as to what he or she provides the editor for the transitioning or bridging of scenes from one to another, is many times the defining line that separates the experienced from the novice.

Many new to industry no/low budget DPs or those that enter into the indie-biz from the ENG (Electronic News Gathering) documentary style cinematography have a propensity to shoot the action and or dialogue only. If filming the action only, there comes a time where there'll be a lack of footage for the editor to work with.

To help blend scenes together there may need to be extra footage that creatively bridges one scene to the next. This so called bridge can be a camera move such as a crane shot, dolly shot, pan, pedestal or a simple tilt of the camera. This is a motion picture medium, not a still photography medium. That statement alone suggests the camera should move as well, and not just on the action. Example:

The scene begins with Monica and James exiting the bistro. They stop on the sidewalk and kiss each other goodbye, then they turn and walk away going opposite directions. The camera is mounted on a crane and, on action, the camera crane slowly raises and pulls back, exposing more of the sidewalk below. As the camera comes close to its final position (2nd position) high in the sky, the camera tilts up and pans towards the busy city street off in the distance. Depending on where the story goes from there, the crane move could provide a smooth transition to the next scene. The bridge offers the editor options, in other words, more to work with. Rather than cutting or dissolving from one scene to the next, a camera move that leads into the action and/or exits the action is just another technique that helps tell the story.

Note: Action sequences such as chase scenes and/or fight scenes, for example, don't require bridge shots, as they would slow down the fast paced sequential action that's ever so necessary for those kinds of scenes.

A particular morning during the "Under the Walnut Tree" production had our lead character chained to the walnut tree and sitting in the dirt awaiting her action cue. Even though we weren't quite ready for action, there was a moment that would have been academy award winning if the DP would have captured what she was doing. In the story the girl has been chained to the tree for days by the time this particular scene takes place. She's filthy dirty, despondent and her spirit is broken. While she was sitting there waiting for "Action", she was looking down and playing with a bug or something. She was completely oblivious to what was going on around her. If only the DP had tilted the camera straight up into the tree limbs, began the camera roll, then slowly tilted the camera down to our actress and stayed on her while she was off in la-la land. That was a moment that was priceless and would have provided for the editor some awesome footage. There were countless situations such as this that were never captured. Very unfortunate, but very typical for a novice DP.

Cranes, dollies, pedestals, pans and tilts many times define a style that is exclusive to a DP's particular artistic expression. Just like with lighting design, they can also become a DP's artistic signature. There is much more to DPing than just capturing the action. Camera movement helps tell the story in a much more interesting way. Think of cranes, dollies, pans and tilts as seasoning for the visual; just as carrots, potatoes, onions and corn are seasonings for a roast. Just a thought…

Rain, Wind and Lightning

The storm has been relentless all night. The heavy non-stop rain and howling fifty-mile-per-hour winds are nothing short of biblical. The wind drives the huge drops of water into the window as if they are clear acrylic bullets fired from a machinegun. As the rivers of water flow down the panes like liquid glass, they create reflections on Angie's face that appear as ghostly tears, whispering Dan's goodbye. Angie stands motionless as she clutches Dan's bloodied shirt. She watches intently as the gurney slowly wheels down the walkway. Flashes of red and blue lights mirrored in her tear-filled eyes tell the story of the tragedy that took place that night. Suddenly a brilliant flash of lightning breaks her concentration. It is then she slowly turns away from the window and walks away... And cut, that's lunch everyone. We're moving on to scene fifty-two, good work everybody...

It is, without a doubt, much cheaper to write a scene than it is to film a scene. In no/low budget independent film making terms, with every scene there is already a strict budget to adhere to. For example, in the above scene, consider the emergency vehicles, flashing red and blue lights, rain, wind machines lightning and an abundance of other lighting instruments, which all add up. "Oh my gosh, this is going to cost a fortune!" However, when considering production value, it's scenes such as these that can have a huge payoff.

Atmospheric effects can add a lot to the production value. A little rain, wind, lightning and viola, the scene is more interesting to watch, not to mention the fact that the audience will be impressed by the fact you had more than a Lowel kit in your back pocket. As long as scenes such as these are kept fairly tight, atmospheric effects can be achieved fairly easily and cheaply if planned properly. In other words, not all atmospheric special effects scenes have to cost a fortune.

Let's start with wind. A high output axial fan is plenty powerful, compact, and it plugs into the wall. For small set-ups they work great. They can be rented from any equipment rental establishment for just a few dollars. By positioning an EMT strobe-fire emergency light-bar that has been mounted to a C-Stand just outside the window, this will create the reflection of the emergency vehicle lights as reflected in our actress's eyes. Small back window light bars can be purchased on-line and they aren't very expensive. Because these strobes aren't very powerful, they may need to be positioned fairly close to the window. Also, because they are designed to operate using 12-volt car power, a 12-volt converter may be required if using house power; otherwise a car battery will be required. Next we must create lightning. Using an HMI with FX shudders attached to the front is the safest way to achieve the effect; however, a strategically placed arc welder can make for some realistic looking lightning as well. Just make sure there is a qualified arc welder operator to make lightning happen. Last but not least, it's the all important rain effect. Hydrant permits aren't very expensive; however, fire hoses and rain towers are. Again keeping the scene fairly small, a nozzle mounted to a garden hose will work just fine. Remember, if the camera is positioned inside only, the raindrops simply have to be blown into the window via the wind machine to mimic a huge storm. By mounting the hose and nozzle to a Cardellini and C-Stand, the makeshift unit can be positioned just outside the window, out of the camera's view. The nozzle should be pointed straight up and far enough from the window to allow the drops of water to fall naturally just in front the window. Using the wind machine to blow the water drops into the glass will create the great storm-of-the-century look. Note: rain must be backlit for the camera to properly capture the effect. Also, time will have to be allotted for the wetting down of the background, i.e. sidewalk, walkway and street, in other words, everything in camera view.

For the exterior lighting, a couple of 1200 PAR HMIs and a few other tungsten heads will be necessary. One HMI would be used for the lightning gag and the other would be used to mimic a street lamp. The other tungsten heads could be used for porch lights and any other background aesthetics such as lighting shrubbery and/or background structures, which adds depth to the scene. For the EMT truck that is parked out front, along with the use of their gurney, they can be borrowed fairly easily, as long as they're not kept there too long.

From inside, the view is spectacular. The torrential rains, the hurricane force winds, and the flashes of lightning all easily create the storm look, all on a shoestring budget. Everything else is performance.

A production I had worked on several years back was an atmospheric special effects extravaganza. Out of thirty-one days of principal photography, we had twenty-nine days of movie rain. Constantly wet, and always cold, the production was as uncomfortable as wearing a Jello suit. A local special effects team was hired to provide the massive amounts of rain required by the production. Hundreds of feet of fire hose, rain towers and heavy duty rain gear were the norm for the many days and nights of filming. The director wanted rain and rain he had. Careful planning and proper budgeting were the keys to making it all work.

Creating scenes that include atmospheric special effects such as rain, wind and lightning can be a huge plus when it comes to adding production value.

"Now… Plus it"
Walt Disney

THE DIRECTOR'S ROLE

I purposely placed the director's chapter at the end of this section, before delving into the technological side of movie making, for good reason. The success of the entire production hinges on this one individual's ability to take charge. With a majority of the many other film making factors behind us, you now have a good idea what the director must contend with when attempting to conquer this complex position. The way in which one executes this role, while subjective in so many aspects, will be a large determining factor when it comes to the success of most, if not all, productions.

Probably the most demanding individual is the no/low budget independent film director. Usually self-appointed, he or she has transformed him or herself from writer to visual storyteller. They have chosen, for whatever reason, to be the captain of their own ship. Sailing on to brighter horizons or sinking into the dark abyss, the production ultimately rides on their ability to command. Not members of the DGA (Directors Guild of America) "yet", they are many times very new to the industry. They have come up through the ranks via Burger King, Blockbuster, lots of books and/or film school to do but one thing, write and direct their very own production. They have the desire to not only create, but to lead and inspire, and hopefully do so without going into some egomaniacal tirade as if possessed by the spirit of an unruly three year old. The director not only sets the stage for the actors, but he or she also has the responsibility of setting the pace and mood for the entire production team. To be a no/low budget film director requires one to assume a multitude of responsibilities. Along with directing the show, he or she must also act as psychologist, consultant, referee and unfortunately, babysitter, all without jeopardizing his or her own integrity.

Writer/Director, One in the Same

Every director, young or old, male or female has their own distinct approach to the art of directing. For the no/low budget bunch, it's usually the writer who has become the director. They see the story being told a certain way and they want to direct it that way. Unfortunately, it's the lack of directing experience that many times contributes most to a production spinning out of control. They have to learn the art of properly communicating and executing their desires and they lead their projects with a compulsion derived from a kind of creative ownership.

Writers who cross over to the directorial camp are becoming more popular these days. Good, bad or indifferent, this epidemic is not going to slow down anytime soon. For those who are to become the next Michael Bay of movie making, it is important to understand that unless well disciplined, this can be the challenge that quickly admits one to an insane asylum. The new-to-industry writer who has made the decision to become the director often finds him or herself suffering from compulsive possessive connection disorder. In other words, they have a connection to their project that can render them immobile or fixated on just one process or approach to achieve a particular outcome. It's kind of like seeing the production through a toilet paper tube. They become oblivious to other possible ways of handling challenges.

During the "Under the Walnut Tree" production we had a park scene, which involved two children who were approximately four years of age. Neither of the children had a lick of acting experience. Their first performance for us, which took place a few weeks prior, was painfully arduous. That being said, there was little hope things would be any different this time around. The scene at the park opened with their character mother, who hasn't seen her kids in months, and is granted visitation with them now that she is clean and sober. With light dialogue and a few blocking moves at the play structure, it should have been a walk in the park, no pun intended. Not even close. For these little guys to hit their mark twice in one set-up was like demanding them to dismiss all laws of gravity and hover. Yet the director continued to make the same demands of the children that weren't ever going to happen. Soon the day came for our fourth trip back to the same location, same scene, same kids, same dialogue and same blocking. The fact was that the script should have been rewritten after the first disastrous attempt. Also, with a few creative changes in camera angles, the story could have been told from a slightly different perspective. In other words the scene would have delivered the same message, just a different approach as to how it was told.

Being the director for a script that one has written can be a very slippery slope. It can be difficult to direct it because of the motherly attachment to the story. One has a preconceived idea as to how it must be done and he or she won't consider it done any other way. If you're the writer/director and you find yourself not being able to visualize the many other possibilities, get advice from someone else. There just might be an easier way to tell the same story. To his credit, the "Under the Walnut Tree" director did finally make the necessary changes to the script and we did get the park scene shot.

Director or Dictator

The director is, for all intents and purposes, the quintessential control freak, which raises the question, is his or her lust for ultimate control of the universe a bad thing? No, otherwise their backsides would never grace the canvas bottom of the director's chair. However, the best of the best of control freaks have learned to command with unassuming, non-threatening power. Good directors have learned to lead without letting on they're actually leading. They demand without being demanding. Their composure precedes them, and their wisdom is their counsel. In clandestine fashion, they know what they want and they know how to get it. Never raising a decibel or fracturing a relationship, the respect they receive is always earned.

The director is the big cheese, the one person who has a finger on the pulse of the entire production. However, like with any position, there are good directors and there are bad directors. Just like in all walks of life, there are those directors who have bad character flaws. The number one bad character trait is: "I'm important and I'm going to make sure everyone knows it." They are the ones who typically become the nemesis of their own production, the director everyone hates. It is this character trait that fuels their power thirsty, egocentric draw to the position of directing in the first place. They are the ones who make sure everyone on the planet knows they are the big cheese and they seem to have more interest in control than they do creativity. They are about as much fun to work with as a nest of angry hornets. This is not to say that this type of director puts out bad work, quite the contrary. Often their work rocks. They're just no fun to work with.

A few years back a young wannabe director was attempting to "wow" someone in Hollywood with a story he had written. A UPM friend of mine asked if I'd be interested in bringing my truck and expertise to the one-night production to help out. I kindly obliged as I was promised it would be an easy shoot, great food and again "lots of fun". In other words, I'd be doing this for free. When I arrived I was immediately whisked away to the back of the house. The spectacular view overlooked a beautiful moonlit lake, four hundred feet below. Steep wooden steps led would-be lake goers down to the private dock. It was on that dock the scene was to take place. A small generator and a cornucopia of lights had to be carried down the rotting wooden steps, one item at a time, with no help. As the torrential rain came down in sheets all night long, it was plain to see, this was not going to be the easy shoot I was promised.

The director, who was maybe twenty years old at best, had hired a prominent DP and a well-known Hollywood actress, very impressive. Sporting bobby pins in his weirdo-looking hairdo, he took charge like a young Napoleon Bonaparte. Firing off orders one right after another, I thought, wow, who is this guy? I was finally introduced to the young dictator. "Hi, my name is K."

"K," I said, "Is that short for something like Ken or Kevin or...?"

"Just K," he barked.

"Okay, K. I'm Rick. I'm the gaffer, nice to meet you."

"Yeah whatever, I need you down there on the dock, where the work is."

What a charming individual.

After a couple of hours of filming, we hiked back up the steep wooden walkway to the top, to warm up and get dry. As I reached the top, a lady kindly offered me a Rice Crispy cookie and a half-cup of lukewarm coffee. How nice of her to offer, yum. I eagerly accepted her offerings. I was so hungry I could have eaten the tray she was carrying. Without hesitation she began hollering down the steep steps. "Kenny, Kenny, honey do you want some cookies?" It was at that time the high-exalted, hokey-finokey director who referred to himself as "K", hollered back.

"Mom, I told you, I go by K."

"I'm sorry honey. K, I have some cookies up here for you, do you want some?"

I can be pretty sure his directorial days have long since passed. It was, no doubt, a one-time fling, funded by his super rich parents. They most likely paid for the Hollywood actress and the award winning DP, all in an attempt to entertain their spoiled-rotten, baby boy's desire of becoming a big-time director. The rest of us flunkies got bupkis; Rice Crispy cookies and pee-warm coffee. While their son got to play Spielberg for a day, the rest of us were treated like pre-Civil War cotton farmers.

Here was a kid who was more interested in power and control than he was creativity. If he had just brought us all together to share with us his desire and direction for the project, I'm sure the production would have gotten him exactly what he wanted, including a little respect. His approach to directing was juvenile and counterproductive. The entire night was laced with temper tantrums and condescending remarks, as if that made him more important. Did K end up in the cold black lake by accident, or was it by intention? I guess we'll never know.

We all accept bad behavior from time to time when working on the no/low budget set. We fully understand it's the nature of the beast. However, there are no big paychecks that sport over-time and meal penalties, which make it easy for cast and crew to dismiss such childish behavior. That being said, a periodic dose of respect and courtesy may be all that separate a mouth that has teeth, from the mouth that has no teeth.

Inspiring the Psychological

I was working as best boy electric on a fairly big Hollywood movie production several years back and was shocked to hear the words "that's a wrap" after only five hours into the day. Because of the location and the fact we were scheduled to be there another week, it was a walk-away set. In other words, we didn't have to pack up any equipment; we simply got to go home. It wasn't until a few days later I had a chance to speak briefly with the "fairly prominent" Hollywood director. I asked him what went wrong in order to cause the early wrap a few days back? "Nothing," he said. "The cast and crew were in need of a little break and I thought that was as good a time as any to make it an early day." I'd never heard of such a thing, at least at that time. Come to find to find out, he did this quite often. Talking with him again at the wrap party, this time in greater detail, he explained the psychological ramifications behind his actions. Being an episodic TV star from a couple of decades prior, he experienced first-hand the results of abusively long, tedious hours on the set. He saw what it did to both cast and crew. It was then he made the decision that when the time came for his turn in the director's chair, he would take a more compassionate, psychological approach towards the position.

Believe it or not, this sort of thing does happen from time to time. Planned as a kind of psychological treat for the cast and crew, its goal is to boost morale and stimulate creative energy, thereby guaranteeing a much more cohesive set in return. I have had the opportunity to work on more than a few projects that have planned schedules with short days here and there, just for that very reason.

A UPM who I've known for a long time showed me on paper how that kind of planning actually saves the production money. By scheduling an extra full day of principal photography and then separating that full day into two separate half- days, which end just short of the first meal, the production gets a full day of production for less money. For one, there's no hot meal to pay for, and second, if properly scheduled, the equipment rental has already been factored in for the week's rental, making for a free day of equipment use. Hence, more gets done with a lot more smiles and for fewer dollars.

Good directing requires balance between creativity and control. If the director has no creative energy, the director will not take the time to demand the best performances possible. If too much creativity is the driving force, one simple scene can take days or even weeks to shoot. Not enough control, and the set becomes a free-for-all, and everyone begins directing; too many chiefs and not enough Indians. Over control and the set becomes a Nazi war camp. Mutiny then becomes a grave possibility.

Consider the old saying, "You can catch more flies with honey than you can with vinegar." A smooth, cohesive, evenly paced production is always more productive than one that is high stress, hard driving, and Gestapo-run. Consider the fact that this is an industry that brings many different types of individuals together. With thirty to forty egos, all the size of mountains, running around on the set fifteen hours a day, six days a week, it's a wonder people don't die. Begin a project with Day One as a fifteen-plus hour day, and watch the project hit the wall before it has a chance to get off the ground. Planning the first day or two to be somewhat shorter than normal does a lot to help meld the many creative egos together more smoothly. Try getting onto the freeway at 70 miles per hour during rush hour traffic and see how far that gets you. The creative arts industry demands much from its cast and crew and when everyone within the hierarchy works smoothly together, it's for the greater good of the project.

The director demands perfection from both cast and crew, and that's just the way it is or at least should be. Any director who accepts less is in the wrong business. Only on a couple of occasions have I ever heard a director respond to a take with, "Good enough, let's move on," as if they'd rather be at home drinking beer. For the young beginner seeking a career as a card-carrying DGA director, learning how to acquire class "A" performances that are worthy of awards, should be goal number one. Since a plethora of takes do not guarantee the coveted academy award, what does? What's a director to do when performances fall flat and character portrayal is nothing more than disconnected, non-compelling and uninteresting?

Every trick in the bag has been used when trying desperately to achieve the highest standard in performance. I've witnessed many directors perform their craft using all different kinds of tactics, some good and some not so good. More often than not, it's those who use the psychological communicative method who seem to have the greatest success.

The Hitler approach to demanding perfection may be entertaining, but I can't say anything positive has ever come from those who use that particular tactic. If irritating and aggravating the cast and crew is the goal, then yes, the Hitler approach can be effective.

The Actor Factor

I was talking with the director for the "Under the Walnut Tree" production shortly after a heated moment took place with one of the actors. He turned to me and with both hands he grabbed his head and said, "I can't get her to do what I want her to do."

As mentioned before, it's easy for a writer/director to become imprisoned by their own preconceived ideas about how the story must be told. The same holds true for actors. They sometimes bring preconceived ideas about how their character should respond to a given situation. Even with good intentions, these ideas may not be in line with what the director has envisioned for that character. In the case of the Walnut Tree production, the actor came with preconceived ideas on how her character should respond and she would not let go of those notions. The director had his hands full trying to shape this actor's performance to best fit the character "He" envisioned.

One must ask the question, why is a "difficult to work with actor" cast in the first place? Was his or her diva-type personality known in advance, and if so, why on earth would someone cast such a person? Some actors are just perfect for the part, no one else will do. And whatever odd personality traits they may bring to the production are justified by their perfect portrayal of the character.

In the no/low budget movie-making world, this is usually not the case. Finding actors who can deliver lines without peeing on their shoes is sometimes considered an award winning performance. That being said, there should never be an actor hired for any no/low budget film who would come to a project with diva-type egomaniacal issues. They aren't stars yet. Nevertheless, one should still get to know those who may be considered for the parts as much as possible. It doesn't take much to do a little research on someone of interest. If they're being considered for a major part, they should have a resume. Check the person out and find out what they were like to work with on past projects. If they were a pain to work with in the past, it's a fair assumption they will be a pain to work with in the future. There are very few no/low budget type actors who are so absolutely perfect for a part that one would consider putting up with any ego-driven idiosyncrasies for even a minute.

As far as our little diva on the "Under the Walnut Tree" production, she actually turned out to be the right person for the part. There was no one who could have played the part as well as she did, regardless of her hard to work with personality. To the director's credit, he continued to keep his cool and in fact got the performance he desired.

The "Actor Factor" is so many times underestimated or completely dismissed as non-relevant. Is an actor who is being considered competent enough to play the part in the first place? Can they deliver their lines, hit their marks and follow directions? Or, is the actor a performance-challenged moron who should stay with flipping burgers? It is difficult for any director, not to mention a novice director for a no/low budget independent film, to be absolutely sure he or she has indeed cast the perfect person for the part. One can only hope. The sad fact is the no/low budget film usually doesn't have the kind of budget that allows for the casting of tried and true Hollywood pros, save for maybe the one or two ringers. Even then, one can't be too sure.

The producers of an independent no/low budget movie I had worked on several years ago had cast the lead singer of a popular heavy metal band for a small day part. It was an attempt to bring a ringer onto the project. The guy was in his mid-fifties sporting long, dyed jet-black hair and skintight leather pants. He burst in the door at his call time and with his heavy English accent, he demanded to know where was his motor home, fifth of Jack Daniels and quart of chocolate milk? By 11:00 AM he was so smashed he couldn't walk, let alone talk. He was a complete waste of skin. Needless to say, he was on a plane back to Scarborough the next day.

During the early stages of pre-pre-production for a screenplay I had co-written with a good friend of mine, we had a meeting with our hopeful director and UPM. It was immediately decided that a ringer or two would be cast to help guarantee distribution. I was previously introduced to a prominent actor who was in town and was pleased to hear he was available and willing to play a part for us; however, the UPM adamantly disapproved as he'd had past experiences with this particular actor. The stories he told about this actor were not at all favorable. In fact he reportedly cost another production thousands of dollars. I was more than stunned, as I'd heard nothing but great things about the guy. As it turned out, the UPM who had discouraged the use of this individual had worked with him some time prior to his stay at Betty Ford. The director friend of mine, who introduced me to and suggested him, had his experiences with him after his rehabilitation, which were very favorable. So what to do? My co-writer partner brought up something that couldn't be argued with. What if this guy falls off the wagon during the middle of our production, and we're forced to retrieve him from some Buenos Aires bar after a three day drinking binge? Point well taken. We weren't willing to take that risk.

The casting process is, by design, the time in which the right person for the right part is determined. At least that is the goal. However, there are times an actor can perform like a seasoned pro during the audition, only to completely fall apart on the set.

While working on a national pizza commercial some years back, the lead actress who was cast to play the part of the mother of three hungry teenage boys turned out to be an absolute train wreck. It was painful to watch as this lady mutilated line after line. Thirty-plus takes later, she only got worse. It got to the point where she started crying, non-stop. That was fun to watch, and after that little show, she was then put back into make-up for another hour, wasting even more valuable time. No one was amused. Even the three boys playing her children were calling their agents. Shot on 35mm film, that single day was more expensive than some independent feature length films. The director/cameraman had to figure out a way to shoot around her. Here was an actor who nailed the audition, she performed the part flawlessly. However, once she was placed in front of the camera with client, ad agency and crew all looking on, she choked. This proves that no one can ever be too sure.

There are only two ways to combat dismal performance syndrome. One is to spend serious time reading the hopefuls during the casting process. If it takes ten call backs, so be it. Try as hard as possible to cast the right people into the appropriate parts. The other is rehearsal time. It's a foregone conclusion that if there is no rehearsal time set aside during pre-production, rehearsal time will take place on the day of filming. That's like learning how to fly at ten thousand feet. No director, experienced or not, can afford that kind of last minute tactic. It's much too costly. Rehearsals are a must and should take place long before principal photography begins. For the writer/director, it's the first time he or she sees their work transformed from the written word to a walking, talking, breathing live performance. Rehearsal time is also the time when bugs can be worked out of the script, at least those that are obvious. And, last but not least, it's a good time for the actor to begin, early on, to develop his or her character.

There are directors who require a multitude of takes for many different reasons; yet, if the right person has indeed been cast and there has been ample rehearsal time, thirty-eight takes should not be the case. Multiple takes do nothing but wear down the actor's energy, causing their performance to deteriorate. Once they begin the crash and burn process, there is no getting back the performance worthy of a print. So many times I've heard directors say to their talent, "That was perfect, let's go again." Before long its take fifteen and nothing has changed, at least for the better. Once an actor has given what would be considered a good performance, get the safety and move on.

The director's approach to working with talent is, like with many things in the performing arts business, very subjective. All directors have different means by which they pull out the performance they're looking for; however, it is the spontaneity and realism of a performance that should be the ultimate goal. Some performances are going to be picture perfect on the first or second take while others are going to require a little more finessing, given a particular situation, of course. As mentioned, there are plenty of books and classes on the subject of directing. I suggest studying the art of directing to its fullest, if that is indeed the career choice desired.

The director is the captain of the ship, so to speak. He or she has the final word. While some directors may ask the arbitrary question, "What did you think?" They are usually asking for praise, not suggestions. There is but one director on the set. That means only one person speaking with the talent, directing the talent and taking charge of the talent. The director, who has learned to communicate his or her intensions effectively to the talent, will typically experience the greatest success.

Communication Skills Required

Recently, a production designer friend of mine and I were talking about some of our past on-set experiences. She told me about a director who would keep important information to himself. He would then use that clandestine knowledge as power over cast and crew. The director thought that by keeping pertinent information secret, he would better maintain his power and control over the set. "I wanted red flowers on that table not purple. Are you that much of an idiot you weren't able to read my mind? Get off my set." This may sound facetious, but this kind of power play nonsense does take place from those who have control issues. As mentioned before, this is not directing, this is merely playing the part of ruler. Big difference.

It is true that some information must be kept secret as it may have some relevance towards drawing a particular reaction from an actor during a scene. However, most film business information must be shared and expressed clearly with all associated departments. No one should be left in the dark. After all, what good can come from playing, "I've got a secret" on the set?

The other end of the spectrum is the "open forum suggestion box" approach to directing or keying a department, which can be just as detrimental. There is but one director and one department head in each category. Having a free-for-all suggestion pool on how something should be accomplished will not only waste time, but severely diminish any authority for those who are in charge. If a department head requests suggestions from time to time, great. That proves the person is confident, flexible and willing to take into considerations other possibilities. Just like with the director, there is but one "Key" for each department. It is by their authority the team is led. As long as the "Key" individual can efficiently and effectively communicate his or her desires and needs for the production, then job well done.

The art of practicing good communication skills, especially in this business, cannot be stressed enough. There is little room in the no/low budget independent film-making world for third grade secret-keeping. There is much to be done and we all must work together. Total interaction and communication between all departments, and of course the director, can only streamline the film making process.

The Cost of Too Much Too Late

It's a foregone conclusion that film days will spin out of control from time to time. During days such as these, it is common for much of the creative inspiration, energy and motivation to be transformed into dissent, confusion and irritation. Cast and crew are exhausted and nothing will suffice but a hot shower and a warm bed. One would think that "too much too late" would persuade the inevitable, the call to wrap. But no, we must persevere and get the last scene in the can. If it's for a good reason, such as location limitations, then great. If, on the other hand, it's to get caught up because of lack of schedule keeping, then that's another story.

While filming a scene for "Under the Walnut Tree", it was the last night of the night schedule, and there was one more scene to get in the can before daybreak. It had already been a tedious night of filming, and still ahead, were more elaborate lighting set-ups, intricate blocking and heavy performance demands. The director's push was on. It is sometimes best to just call the day, enough is enough. Remember, without storyboards or at the very least, shot lists, a schedule can easily get of control and that's exactly what took place this time.

The following evening while watching the dailies in the production office, it became apparent that the last scene from the night before wasn't going to work. The acting was horrific and many of the shots were out of focus. The decision to push on may have seemed to be the right thing to do at the time, but it didn't work. We had to schedule yet another night for that scene to be re-shot. Not only was too much time spent on previous scenes, too many scenes were scheduled for the night's shooting as well. I cannot stress enough the importance of storyboards and/or shot lists. There must be a concise plan in place that lists each and every shot for a given scene. Once the plan is in place it must be followed, and that's where having a good "First Assistant Director" comes into play.

The First Assistant Director

Before moving on from the director chapter, the position of the First AD (First Assistant Director) must also be addressed. In a sense, a misnomer by title, the First AD does not have any directorial responsibilities per se. However, this job is so vitally important to the daily progress of a production. It cannot be stressed enough that such a position must be filled by someone who truly knows his or her craft.

The First AD is many times mischaracterized as the bad guy, the one individual who's described as the big "A-hole" on the set. This is not generally a true fact. I know my fair share of First ADs and they are generally good people. They have a job to do and that is to keep the production moving along at a steady, productive pace. When crew members are found sitting on apple boxes smoking cigarettes, drinking coffee and chit-chatting the day away, most assuredly the First AD is going to be the Big Dog who gets them back to work.

Get two, three or, fifty creative types on the set and the day quickly goes away much like toilet paper on a bonfire. Directors and DPs, along with other department heads, can often go into major "tweak" mode during the preparation of a scene. In other words, left to their own, they'll eat up the entire day finessing lights, dressing and redressing the set, blocking and rehearsing actors, and fussing with anything else they can find. The First AD will ensure all departments stay on task and on schedule.

Last but least, the First AD oversees the talent and knows of their whereabouts at any given time. He or she is the Head Cheese who will make sure talent is on set promptly and in front of the camera when needed. Many times the First AD will have a PA or two to help in the retrieval of both actors and extras. Time is the most valuable, irreplaceable commodity we have. The First AD's claim to fame is to drive the production so precious time is not wasted.

"Adversity is the Stone on Which I Sharpen My Blade"
Author Unknown

Part Two

Intro

The next chapters are dedicated to the many sciences associated with film style photography, which include lighting and other on-set technical applications. Some are simple procedures that, by design, work for even the lowest of budgets. From the muddy, grainy images of the first consumer-grade video cameras of yesteryear to the 35mm high-def digital cameras of today, technology has brought us to a point never before dreamed of. It is now possible to create imagery that very closely mimics the look of film, and for less than the cost of a used car. This much sought after career has never before been so attainable for so many.

Even though the same tried and true movie making procedures and principles that have been around for decades haven't changed much, technology has. The independent filmmakers from the past have witnessed first-hand this amazing technical progression. From expensive film to clumsy videotape to the tiny memory card, motion picture imagery has never been easier to capture all while looking so remarkable. Tight space camera set-ups are a breeze because the cameras of today are no larger than a block of cheddar cheese, and dailies are as easy as a simple click of the mouse. That being said, the basic sciences that make up motion picture photography will probably never change. It is the knowledge and understanding of these technical factors that are the creative foundations for the visual story telling medium.

Chapter Nine

THE DP and the INDIE-CAMERA

On the premise that we all wish to create artfully composed story-telling imagery, it all starts with the understanding of the camera and its functions. The days of the event-gathering videotape cameras of yesteryear are long behind us, at least for movie making. Thank the good Lord for that; however, even back then lighting was a necessary evil that had to be taken into consideration. Unfortunately, when lighting instruments weren't available, it was the iris control that became way too handy.

The Master Lighting Control Valve

For any type of photography, lighting is everything, and there never seems to be enough, at least for the no/low budget bunch. That is why the iris has often been used as a lighting control device. From years past, the iris ring was, and still is today, considered to be more of a brightness control than a true aperture f-stop control. First and foremost, and without equivocation, the iris is not, nor should ever be considered the master lighting control valve for the DP who desires to go beyond the ranks of wedding videographer. The onset of the very first consumer grade video cameras to hit the market during the late seventies and early eighties gave birth to a whole new breed of wannabe independent filmmakers. However, it was also at that time the basic rules of cinematography, such as the photographic triangle, went out the back door like a bad dog. In other words, the launch of the consumer grade video camera gave birth to wannabe filmmakers that didn't have to know much, if anything at all, about the true art of cinematography.

As the "Under the Walnut Tree" production began, I was not privy early on to the experience level of the crew I would be working with. It wasn't until we began principal photography I learned of the lack of technical experience on the set. Here was a young writer/director who writes amazing scripts being forced to rely heavily on a DP with very limited film camera knowledge. The DP was new to the industry, lacking the necessary technical knowledge required for using a 35mm Hi-definition camera. The new DP had to deal with exposure, DOF (depth of field), focal points, film speeds and other factors that make for today's filmography. This was unfortunately out of his ENG (Electronic News Gathering) video background.

There's much one must know when capturing imagery with the digital "Hi-def 35mm indie-cameras" of today. The science and knowledge required for the proper use of film cameras has finally come into play for the no/low budget indie film crowd. Just like with Hollywood's 35mm film cameras, today's hi-def digital cameras sport interchangeable lenses with true operational f-stop rings, that bring to the program DOF and focal point concerns, all of which play a huge part in the image gathering process. The days of relying on the iris for lighting are over.

The Lens Factor

Unlike yesterday's video cameras, complete with fixed mount lenses, continuous-spin focus rings, electronic zoom control and auto iris, today's indie-cameras are much more sophisticated. The new 24 frames per second, high definition resolution digital cameras are actually designed with the independent filmmaker in mind.

The high-def digital camera with its interchangeable lenses redefines the creative processes available to today's filmmaker. With 35mm sensors and prime lenses to match, some of the greatest images ever can now be experienced at a comparatively low cost.

The first factor that must be taken into consideration when taking advantage of interchangeable lenses is the wide-open f-stop rating given for a particular lens. In other words, is the lens a slow lens or is it a fast lens? The speed of a lens is determined by the wide-open aperture size of the lens and is rated by f-stop i.e. *f*-1.4... *f*-2.8... *f*-4 etc. A lens that sports a lens speed designation of *f*-2.8 would be considered a slower lens than that of an *f*-1.4 lens. Simply put, the *f*-1.4 lens has a larger aperture opening at the widest *f*-1.4 setting than that of an *f*-2.8 lens set to its widest setting, allowing for more light to enter. So what are the advantages and disadvantages of the slower and faster lenses?

First, it is important to look at the maximum light value or exposure value given to the two exampled lenses. The amount of light it will take for a normal exposure value will need to quadruple for an *f*-2.8 lens compared to that of an *f*-1.4 lens. If you think of f-stops as fractions, it will be easier to understand. (*"f" equals focal length divided by 1.4, 2.8, 4, 5.6 etc.*) Note: As the f-stop number increases (stopping down), the amount of light required increases. This is also referred to as the halving and doubling principle. An f-stop of *f*-2.8 requires half the light than that of an f-stop of *f*-4, whereas, an f-stop of *f*-4 requires double the light required by that of an f-stop of *f*-2.8. Let's go one step further. Let's say, for example, we have two 24mm lenses that are separated only by aperture size. One lens sports a widest aperture setting of *f*-1.4 and the other the widest opening is *f*-2.8. Broken down, there is a difference of two stops between *f*-1.4 and *f*-2.8 (*f*-1.4 to *f*-2.0 is one stop... *f*-2.0 to *f*-2.8 is another stop, for a total of 2 stops). It will require four times the amount of light using an *f*-2.8 lens at its widest f-stop setting than that of the faster lens of *f*-1.4 set at its widest setting.

Here's the rub: it may take half the light to achieve an equal exposure value using the faster f-1.4 lens; however, the faster lens set at the widest f-1.4 stop also means a much shallower depth of field.

The Photographic Triangle

Filming a scene with an f-1.4 lens wide open as opposed to using an f-2.8 lens, also wide open, may seem the way to go as it will require only half the light. The problem is that the depth of field will be so shallow that any forward or rearward movement by either the camera or subject will result in a lot of out of focus footage. Unless the focus puller is really on his or her game, this can be a real problem. The stopping down of the lens or the increasing of the f-stop number will consequently increase the depth of field. Conversely, when the aperture is increased in size from f-4 to f-2.8, the depth of field then decreases. How this translates to the proper choice of lenses can either be a creative tool or depth of field nightmare depending on the situation.

During the pre-production phase of any project, I like to know from the DP, what f-stop he or she would like to use as a base line for their lens aperture setting. This information, along with the overall look and feel of the project, will give me an idea of what kind of lighting package they'll be working with. An f-stop of somewhere between f-2.8 to f-4 is what I generally hope for when working on a no/low budget project. This in-between designation is usually referred to as a "split", in other words a split between f-2.8 and f-4. Pronounced on the set, it would sound like, "two-eight-four split". In other words, the DP desires some flexibility for his or her desired depth of field. The number of instruments and size of lighting instruments will also need to be considered. It is during the pre-production phase that the DP and the gaffer will determine what lighting package will best suit the overall project.

F-stop is only one side of the photographic triangle. There is also shutter speed and film speed to consider. In still photography, shutter speed or the time value given for light to enter through the lens can be adjusted. This adjustment can range from milliseconds to minutes; however, for the motion picture camera this is generally not the case. Obviously, film speed rates can be adjusted for motion picture cameras to accommodate high speed or slow motion effects, but for our purposes we'll be using the normal 24fps (frames per second) for our example. That being said, consider motion picture film being exposed to light at a rate of 24fps. Therefore, should one conclude that 24fps would then equate to a 24th of a second shutter speed? No.

All SLR (Single-lens reflex) cameras have "view through the lens" eyepieces to see what is being captured by either film or sensor. This is accomplished by the incorporation of a mirror mechanism that flips up out of the light path to the film/sensor plain when the shutter is triggered, which explains why what is visible through the eyepiece goes dark for a nanosecond when a picture is being taken. For motion picture film cameras, such as 16mm or 35mm cameras, the same basic principal is applied. However, for the eyepiece to project to the viewer what is being exposed to the film, the mirror is instead a spinning half circle disc mechanism. As the mirror disc spins, its function is to split the light entering the lens equally between the film plane and the eyepiece. Only half of the light that enters the lens goes to the film plane, while the other half goes to said eyepiece. For exposure calculations, this action translates to only half of the 24th of a second. The actual shutter speed measurement computes to 48th of a second or 50th of a second rounded up. Light meters compute shutter speeds at tenths of a second increments; therefore, a 50th of a second reading would be closest to the 48th of a second shutter speed of a 24fps motion picture camera. Not to worry, the 50th of a second setting will be close enough to make any necessary exposure value calculations. This means that in regards to the motion picture camera's 24 frames per second, the (48th) 50th of a second shutter speed would then be a non-variable factor applied to the photographic triangle.

There is one other equation to be factored into the photographic triangle and that is film speed. In the early days of film making, there was only one film speed available, ASA 64. In today's standards, this would be considered a very slow film. So what is film speed? Film speed, in simple terms, is a particular film emulsion's photographic sensitivity to light. The lower the number or photographic sensitivity measurement, the less sensitive the film is to light, conversely the higher the number, the more sensitive the film is to light. In layman's terms, the amount of time necessary for a film's emulsion to be exposed defines the speed of the film. This numeric scale in today's terms is referred to as ISO. The ISO settings on most digital cameras range from 100 ISO and up.

What is the difference between ISO and ASA? The ASA (American Standard Association) numerical scale once used for film speed classifications in the past, was in 1987, combined with its closely comparative, arithmetic scale of the former Soviet Union, along with Britain's much different scale, to form the ISO (International Organization for Standardization) scale we use today. However, all we need to know is the lower film speed or setting number, the slower the film and the less sensitive to light. Conversely, the greater the film speed number or setting, the faster the film, or greater sensitivity to light.

We have now learned that the f-stop, or aperture diameter, determines the amount of light that is exposed to the film plane. And the speed of the film also corresponds mathematically when factoring in the amount of light for said exposure as well. Now let's take those two factors and put them to work in a low light situation.

For our example, we are going to use a fast f-1.4 lens, but we've only stopped down to an f-2.0 due to the amount of light available, while still maintaining some depth of field. However, the action in front of the lens dictates that it's necessary to stop down further to an f-4 to gain even more depth of field. By selecting the faster film speed setting, we can get another two stops, which increases the depth of field while still maintaining the same desired exposure value. For instance, by increasing the selected film speed setting from 100 ISO to 400 ISO, this will add two stops of exposure value allowing us to stop down two stops to an f-stop of f-4.

Again, rather than the f-stop controlling the amount of light for exposure, the f-stop has but one function, "Depth of Field." This means film speed is what controls the amount of light that is exposed to the sensor or digital film plain. This give and take between DOF and exposure value becomes another tool by which the DP can creatively tell the story.

There is the issue of noise or grain artifacts associated with faster film stocks or faster digital film settings. It is true that earlier and less expensive digital cameras do not handle noise/grain very well at higher ISO settings. The more advanced and obviously more expensive indie-cameras produce images that control much better noise/grain artifacts, in fact, up to 400 ISO, with some cameras going higher before noise is indeed noticeable.

If you've ever watched a "behind the scenes" segment commonly associated with a DVD movie, you've, no doubt, noticed how much brighter the scene is that has been captured by the EPK (Electronic Press Kit) video camera compared to the same scene depicted in the movie. There are three main factors for this light value discrepancy. The first is the fact that the "behind the scenes" footage was shot on video. The iris of the video camera has been opened up to capture both the scene as performed and the darker, behind the scene areas. The second factor is, during processing, the film or scene has been processed down. In other words, some of the brightness has been taken down during the processing phase, usually due to creative desires. Lastly, and more likely, the scene was shot on a slow film stock such as 100 ISO for optimum quality, again, less grain. A slow film stock (low numeric ISO rating) will require much more light for proper exposure.

There is a simple experiment you can perform if you have a fairly decent SLR digital camera at your disposal. Note: The camera must allow for manual settings. Set the camera up as such: with the camera securely mounted to a tripod, start with 100 ISO for the film speed, with a 50mm lens. Set the f-stop to an *f*-2.8 – *f*-4 split, and finally set the shutter speed to a 50th of a second. This will emulate a typical single frame of a 24fps 35mm motion picture camera using 100 ISO film stock. Place your subject approximately 5 feet in distance from the focal plane. Using a 300 watt Fresnel, place the light 90 degrees to the side of the subject at approximately 8 feet in distance, in an otherwise dark room. Next, take your first shot. You'll notice how dark the image is compared to how the scene appears to the naked eye. The subject will be lit on one side only and the background and all surrounding areas will fall into the darkness as well, in fact, too dark to depict any outlying detail. Let's continue on with the experiment.

Now, move the light closer to the subject, approximately 12 to18 inches. Take another shot. Repeat the process, continuing to move the light closer to the subject two or three times. You'll notice that even though the subject becomes brighter as the pictures are taken, the background and surrounding areas still remain fairly dark. With the light approximately 18 inches from the subject, the subject will appear over-exposed on the lit side, and the dark side of the face will barely expose some facial features. Still the background of the room remains dark. The low sensitivity of the digital 100 ISO setting will only expose for the subject, mimicking what would be captured on motion picture film with the same 100 ISO.

For our final experiment, we'll move the light back to its starting position. Rather than moving the light closer to the subject to increase exposure value, we'll increase the film speed setting until the subject has an acceptable exposure. (Never mind the noise/grain artifacts as the subject becomes exposed). This experiment shows how the film speed setting can be used to gain exposure without compromising depth of field. However, take notice of the surrounding room within the image; much of the background is also exposed. This is where the rubber meets the road, so to speak. There becomes a balancing act between exposing for the subject while maintaining the desired DOF and then creatively lighting the scene. If the filmsetting is too fast, it will be difficult to creatively paint with light because surrounding background elements, even though exposed, will have a grayish muddy, somewhat weird appearance. A film speed setting that is too slow will severely diminish the depth of field. The only solution to achieving proper exposure values along with maintaining desirable depths of field is to have a substantial inventory of lighting instruments.

Teching the Camera

Time spent preparing the camera and lenses for principal photography is about as important as a surgeon sterilizing his instruments prior to surgery. Granted, no one will die from infection, but one could easily die if the camera and lenses do not function properly on the set. This process is referred to as "teching" the camera.

The camera tech procedure is a function that is performed by the AC. For cameras and lenses that are rented, which is usually the practice for the better funded productions, this procedure is typically conducted in a room that the rental house has set aside somewhere on the premises. The main purpose of teching the camera is to check for proper camera functionality and to calibrate lenses. For film cameras, there are many moving parts, and the proper function of the camera must be checked. For the digital indie-type cameras, this is the time where resolution and color calibrating is done. Also, each lens that is part of the package must be meticulously cleaned and also calibrated. Documenting the lenses for critical focus using focusing/resolution and target charts, must be done at this time as well. For many lenses, the focus distance marks, which are measured in feet and millimeters on the focus ring, can be incorrect. For this reason, each lens is checked for focus at 6-inch intervals and marked accordingly, using white tape on the focus ring part of the lens. When a measurement is taken from the focal plane to the subject, using a tape measuring scale, there is an exact corresponding measurement on the lens, which is vital for DOF calculations and the accurate following of focus procedures.

The biggest problem with some no/low budget productions is that the camera and lens packages, if there is indeed a lens package, are usually owner operated. Again, if the DP comes from wedding world, the ever-so-important "Camera Tech" procedure may be nothing more than checking to see if the camera is indeed in the camera bag, where it was left last.

While trying to capture an action sequence using a camera jib during the "Under the Walnut Tree" production, the AC who was also the focus puller was having trouble maintaining critical focus during a particular camera move. I had suggested we compare the critical focus measurement displayed on the lens with a measuring tape, using a target. As suspected, the focus ring measurement marks did not match actual measured distances via the scale. The focus measurement on this particular lens indicated 3-feet-6-inches at the point of spot-on focus. In actuality, the focal distance from focal plane to subject was actually 5 feet. This discrepancy would have been realized early on during the "camera tech", had there been one, and with proper recalibration documentation marks on the lens, following focus would not have been an issue.

If possible, an industry trained AC should be another priority part of the budget. Having a qualified AC who is responsible for the care of the camera and lenses, is essential to the smooth workings of the production. If a production is not able to hire such a professional, I strongly suggest someone tech-minded be chosen and dedicated to that position. There are plenty of on-line tutorials that are specific to the teaching of teching procedures for today's high-def digital cameras and lenses. Keep in mind, the AC is also responsible for filling out camera reports. We'll be discussing that procedure in more detail later on.

Composing Confidence

Before proceeding, now is a good time to delve into a bit of the psychological again. This time it's the DP's turn on the couch. All the filmmaker techno-knowledge in the world won't add up to much more than a pile of floppy discs if the one behind the camera lacks self-confidence.

Many years ago I overheard a couple of photographers talking. One was a weekend hobby photographer and the other was a seasoned professional. The weekender commented to the pro that he didn't think he had what it takes to become a professional photographer. Of course the professional asked why he thought that. The guy replied, "Even after years of practice, I don't feel I'm able to compose good shots. I'm always second guessing my decisions." A photographer friend of mine does the very same thing. He is always asking me questions about my decision making process. He asks, "How do I decide what size of lens to use and how do I decide what the depth of field will be? How do I choose an angle that best sells the shot?"

Back in the early eighties, while learning how to fly planes, I had a flight instructor who told me of a gentleman student of hers who, even after countless hours of landing instruction, could not land the plane on his own. She finally had to drop him as her student. She said to me, "He just didn't have what it takes to fly." That always bothered me. From that point on, I would often have second-guessing moments questioning whether I really had "it" or not. Did I have the natural-born talent to be whatever, that extra-added dose of magic that makes some of us special? Great, maybe my desire was to be an idiot savant. I'd be able to play piano like a virtuoso, but couldn't walk from here to there without crapping in my pants.

So what is it that makes us really good at something? Besides training, it means putting on the ol' confidence suit. If you've taken the time to learn your craft, then it's time to take the bull by the horns and command yourself to believe in you.

While having a natural born God given talent is certainly a plus, for most of us it has more to do with hard work, learning and practice. You've, no doubt, heard the term, "Fake it, till you make it." There's a lot to be said for that statement. However, you can't fake it till you make it without some kind of training. The famous cinematographer, Dean Semler, didn't just wake up one day with a Panavision camera stuck to his face. He worked hard to get into that position. I honestly believe he saw himself in that position long before "it" actually happened. To get there, I'm positive he studied hard and practiced hard. There is another saying, "The harder you work, the luckier you get." I know my fair share of wannabe cowboys. They wear cowboy hats, cowboy boots, big cowboy belt buckles, Bolo ties and roughrider jeans. They may look the part, but few will ever come face to face with an actual steam-snorting, snot-blowing bull, and I'm sure it they did, they'd run off like a 10-year-old school girl.

Take my photographer friend, for instance. He knows and understands the creative ramifications of the photographic triangle seven ways to Sunday, yet he constantly questions his creative choices and decisions. All of his questions derive from lack of self-confidence. He works hard and knows his craft well. I honestly believe he'd be light years ahead by taking a self confidence class, maybe even seeing a therapist a couple of times a week. He needs to see himself being successful in the role he's playing in life as a photographer. Creativity comes with schooling, practice and hard work. Most famous artists, started as students. Only with knowledge can one begin to experiment.

Creativity is spawned, in part, by experimentation. Take a little of this or that and maybe add some of those, and viola! Pretty soon, with enough information, the floodgates of creative energies open up. Will every idea work? Heck no. In fact, I could write a book on all of the ideas and concepts that don't work; however, once you do find a scenario that looks good and of course works well, stick with that scenario and don't second-guess your decisions. When approaching a particular scene, ask yourself, what's the sell? In other words, what are we trying to sell to the audience? It all comes down to making concrete decisions based on the knowledge you've garnered and the self-confidence you exude. Ask a lot of questions. The more information you have, the fewer chances you'll come off looking like a boob later on.

Composing the Sell Factor

Going back to our bistro scene from a couple of chapters back, let's assume that today we are filming the interior part of our scene. For example purposes, we'll begin the day's filming with the establishing master shots of Monica and James seated at their table. Also, we'll be using a straightforward sequential approach, shooting the scene from widest composition to tightest (close-ups).

I've made mention of this before, but it does deserve repeating. There is a fine line between not enough coverage and too much coverage. That being said, for our scenario let's assume we actually have storyboards to work with. These storyboards will require establishing shot set-ups to be filmed from three different locations within the bistro.

The wide establishing shots introduce the audience to our couple's location, selling to them a setting within a particular place in time. Also the wide establishing shots will give the editor something to cut to just in case there's some snafu such as a missed line, sound bust or other technical issue. The entire table portion of the bistro scene is performed from beginning to end from all three master establishing, wide shot locations. The scene will be performed from beginning to end from each location. While a perfect performance from our lead characters is the goal, there still may be small discrepancies within the scene. Not to worry. It is quite possible for small snafus to be corrected and captured from one of the other camera angles.

With the wide establishing shots completed, we'll now move the camera closer to the action. The MCU, (medium close-up) which in this case may also be referred to as the "two shot" is set up. The camera move will include all necessary lighting adjustments, which will also require a lens change. The MCU will not be so wide as to expose the entire bistro, but wide enough to include both actors equally. In our case, for Monica and James, the MCU will require the camera to be set up perpendicular to the couple's action, in other words, a side shot of the two sitting across from each other at their table. This shot will expose more closely their dialogue and interaction with each other, and with all other subsequent players who were captured during the wide shot. Again the scene is performed from beginning to end just as with the wide shot. It is important to note that all action must be performed identically from set-up to set-up, i.e. if Monica places her right elbow on the table on a particular line during the wide shot, she must do exactly the same every time the scene is performed. Obviously this would be likewise for all characters in the scene.

With the MCU in the can, we can move in for the single shots for each of the characters. These are the close-ups, which are also referred to as "punch-ins." This is the time when the DP, along with the director, will create story-telling compositions that help to motivate audience emotion. Say, for instance, the bistro scene includes the couple's breakup. Certain motivating camera moves along with motivating compositions would be addressed at this time. This would have been determined and referenced on the storyboards long before the day's scheduled filming. Composing a close up for an actor may include a few different set-up possibilities, which brings up the first consideration. Is the close-up composition supposed to be clean or dirty? If the shot is designed to be a clean shot of James, James is the only person seen within the frame. If the shot of James is dirty, the camera would be set up to include a portion of Monica's shoulder and/or a portion of her head. Many times it's both the clean and dirty compositions that are captured, as the camera is in close proximity to easily capturing both.

Creating the "grab the audience" moment, because something important is happening, may require some type of motivating camera move. Say, for instance, James asks Monica for a divorce during the bistro scene. This is where adding a slight dolly move may help motivate the audience. Disclaimer: This is for example purposes only as the following will no doubt come off like a shot from some Lifetime movie.

The story has Monica and James eating lunch. James is abnormally quiet. Monica finally asks James, "What's wrong?" Rather than James blurting out, "Pass me the salt, and by the way I want a divorce," the scene is played more dramatically. James sits there silent for a moment, incorporating his well-practiced William Shatner pause. James slowly sets his fork down, picks up his napkin and wipes his mouth. Clearing his throat and in a nervous voice, he says, "Monica… you know I care about you. I always have, but I want a divorce. I'm in love with Erin, the girl from up the street." He then looks up at Monica and awaits her reaction. While this is happening, the camera is on a steady MCU on him. On the tail end of his line the camera angle cuts to Monica. For this shot, the frame starts off as an MCU on Monica, but slowly the camera dolly push begins. Monica's reaction is magnified ten fold by the slow push into her face. Obviously this is an old school classic textbook shot, but the idea is to help generate emotion.

Many years ago I was hired by a court reporting service to video tape depositions. Depositions are recorded testimonies of witnesses who, for whatever reason, cannot be available on the day of the court hearing. Both the petitioning and defending attorneys will hire video services whenever such situations arise. Most depositions are those of medical doctors, as their schedules are the busiest. They are paid to testify as professional, credible witnesses who, due to their professional opinions, can affect the outcome of a lawsuit. With a motion picture background, composing cool shots for this sort of thing would be right up my alley.

One of my first depositions was that of a doctor hired to testify for a personal injury lawsuit resulting from a car crash. It didn't take long for the defending attorney to ask the doctor if he was being paid for his testimony. The doctor acknowledged the fact that he was indeed being paid as a professional witness; however, it was the following question that sealed his fate. The defending attorney then asked, "How much

is the plaintiff paying you for your so-called expert opinion, Doctor?"
It was at that moment my middle finger on my right hand carefully
began pushing down on the zoom control. Tighter and tighter the
frame became on the doctor's face. I knew I had him. As he patted
the huge beads of sweat from his forehead with his handkerchief,
he finally coughed it up. As I tilted the camera down to expose his
mouth, full screen, he spilled his guts. If only it was in slow motion.
His voice stammered, "Six-hundred dollars," he said. Finally the ol'
Doc was exposed as the charlatan he truly was. Six hundred dollars for
a ten-minute testimony. What a schmuck. Because of my excellent
background in professional camera work, not only would he never
testify again, he would spend the rest of his life behind bars. Ever so
proud, I brought the award winning performance back to the office
for all to see. I had to reschedule with both attorneys and the fine
doctor to re-shoot the whole deposition over again. It was not my job
to create some Perry Mason style courtroom drama. My job was to
simply record his testimony. No bias, no editorializing and certainly
no dramatic camera play. By zooming in on the doctor the way I did,
I completely discredited the poor doctor's testimony. Subtle camera
moves, extreme close-ups and creative compositions are all effective
tools for story telling purposes. Just be careful as to what story it is
you're telling.

Just like with any art medium, the composition or framing of a
shot is also subjective. While there are learned rules of the game, it's
those same rules that are broken all in the name of art. Thirty years ago
lens flare would've gotten most cinematographers fired. Today, lens
flares are considered to be artistic creative highlights of which awards
are now given. To truly know and understand the functionality of the
camera and its lenses will do much to enhance the overall creative
process.

"You don't take a photograph, you make it."

Ansel Adams

Chapter Ten

UNDERSTANDING COLOR TEMPERATURE

Good lighting design is more than exposure and placement; however, lighting also demands serious attention when considering the color of light emitted. The DP must have a working knowledge of these color spectrums of light and how to correctly apply them or correct them. Just like with the artist's pallet and vast assortment of colored paints, so are the many possible colors of light for the cinematographer/DP. However, knowing what kind of light will appear as white light when photographed is the first objective. Photographic lighting has a correlating color value and that color value is measured in Kelvin temperature degrees.

Dr. William Kelvin and the Carbon Experiment

In the mid 1800's, a British mathematician and physicist, William Thomas Kelvin, discovered and created a temperature scale consisting of an absolute zero. This temperature is where molecular energy or movement is at a minimum. The temperature is -273.15 degrees Kelvin, which is in direct correlation to the Celsius scale, (Zero degrees Celsius). Today we mostly use the Fahrenheit scale for measuring temperature; 32 degrees Fahrenheit is freezing and 212 degrees Fahrenheit is boiling. Dr. Kelvin was more interested in the physical science of extreme temperature measurements rather than determining the best temperature for wearing shorts.

Later in the nineteenth century, Kelvin made another interesting discovery. A block of black carbon changes color when heated. The block of black carbon heated in a blast furnace will change color as the temperature increases. The carbon block, when first heated, will begin to glow red, then orange, then yellow, then white and finally blue, as the temperature increases into the thousands of degrees. It was then that each progressive color was assigned a temperature value. Kelvin assigned a correlating color temperature number based on his -273.15 Kelvin temperature scale. Some discoveries, however, come about way before their time. After all, what good was the silicon chip in 1875?

From Black Carbon to Light Bulb

The Kelvin color temperature measurement didn't have much relevance until color film emulsions for motion picture became a serious player within the movie industry. After the novelty age of color film for motion picture, it finally became the industry standard. It was then the various light spectrums recorded on film had to be dealt with more seriously, which made it necessary to better control the color value of light.

Since light has a direct color temperature correlation to Kelvin's super heated carbon block discovery, this would suggest all light be given an equivalent numeric color temperature value. Example: When the heated carbon block approaches approximately 2,500 to 2,900 degrees Kelvin, the color of the carbon will cast a light orange hue. This light orange hue is comparable to a standard household light bulb. Going one step further, motion picture type quartz or tungsten lighting instruments, including some photofloods, are color temperature balanced at, or very close to, 3200 degrees Kelvin (3200K). This is the same color temperature rating given to tungsten film, and also designated to the electronic 3200K degree setting on today's digital cameras. Tungsten film and the tungsten setting is typically used for, but not exclusive to, indoor lighting because tungsten film, or the electronic equivalent thereof, recognizes

3200K degree tungsten light as close to true white light.

In contrast, daylight balanced film is designated for, but not exclusive to, outdoor daytime photography. At 5600 degrees Kelvin, the super-heated block of carbon casts a color that is in the white/blue end of the spectrum. The higher Kelvin temperature rating of 5600 degrees Kelvin (5600K) film and the 5600K digital camera setting is designed for outdoor daytime exposures. Since daylight has a much bluer hue than that of tungsten light, daylight-balanced film stock, or the daylight setting on a digital camera, will create images that are considered to be more natural in appearance for images captured in daylight. Just like with tungsten-balanced film for indoor use, the daylight-balanced film and/or 5600K digital settings will record daylight as true white light for daytime outdoor use.

Color Temperature Correction

Taking the indoor/outdoor color temperature designations a bit further, what if the 3200K and 5600K film stocks or digital settings were reversed? For instance, let's use tungsten film outdoors in daylight and the daylight film indoors with tungsten-balanced lamps. Tungsten film will record daylight in the bluer than natural spectrum and daylight film will record tungsten light as orange. Because there are many instances where the color of light may be mixed within a scene, there is a color correction formula used for necessary color temperature adjustments. This color correction formula is referred to as "Mired Shift."

The word "Mired" acts as an acronym for "Micro Reciprocal Degree." In other words, there is an opposite, correlated color that will bring orange back to true white and blue back to white as well. "Shift" refers to the amount of degrees of correction it will require to convert either daylight 5600K degrees to 3200K degrees tungsten, or vise versa. For example, if white records either blue or orange on film, there will need to be a color shift correction. This will need to be accomplished by either changing the color of light emitting from certain lighting instruments, or correcting the color of ambient light coming in from windows, or filtering the camera's lens and/or changing the film color temperature setting on the camera; or all the above. The objective is to get all light sources to record white as true white, unless there is an artistic motive to do otherwise.

Before addressing the many creative influences this knowledge may bring to the program, it is first important to address the application of color correction in order to obtain proper white color balance. Let's again visit the bistro where we are filming the daytime interior scene with Monica and James. Also for the sake of the example, let's say the bistro happens to be smaller than originally planned, and two sides of the bistro have floor-to-ceiling windows. The owner has allowed us to shoot on Sunday from noon until midnight. The month is March and sunset is approximately at 7:00pm. Daylight coming in through the windows, along with the practical restaurant lighting, is what we have to balance for. Our lighting package includes a few tungsten heads and three HMIs. If we use all tungsten lights to match the practical lamps that are already used in the bistro, and the film's color temperature is set for 3200K tungsten, the interior lighting and tungsten-balanced lighting instruments will record as normal or natural white. However, outside the windows and the light coming in from the outside will appear oddly blue when recorded. If, on the other hand, the camera's color temperature filter is set to daylight, the light coming in from the windows, including everything captured outside the windows, will record normal in color, but now the interior tungsten-balanced lamps will record oddly orange. We must do some color correction.

In simple terms, the main reason for color correcting light is so that an image will appear natural as seen by the audience. There's a simple formula that can be used to determine the amount of mired shift necessary to correct a particular light source. A corrected mired shift measurement is derived by dividing one million by the Kelvin degree temperature of the source. Example: Divide one million by the Kelvin temperature of 5600K degrees (daylight) and this equals 179 degrees of mired shift. This is the amount of degrees it will take to convert daylight 5600K to 3200K degrees tungsten, give or take a few degrees, depending on the manufacturer of color correction material. Likewise, by using the same formula for tungsten light, one million divided by 3200K degrees tungsten equals 313 degrees. By subtracting 179 from 313, the sum of 134 degrees is derived, which is the mired shift measurement necessary to convert tungsten light 3200K to 5600K degrees daylight. Again, the actual color correction degree will be dependent on the manufacturer of the color correction material.

When referring to color correction material, it involves lighting filters or "gels." First it's important to understand that today's indie-cameras have built-in variable color temperature settings. In fact, almost any in-between Kelvin temperature setting can be achieved by simply reprogramming a setting or two; however, it will also be necessary to apply color temperature correction gel to lighting instruments, windows, or both to fine tune the color of light in order to best capture true white.

Gel material is very thin and is manufactured as transparent colored sheets or rolls of plastic. This transparent plastic sheeting is designed to be heat resistant so it can withstand hot lights, while still thin enough to be evenly adhered to windows. Gel material is available and sold by the roll or cut-sheet by grip supply houses from coast to coast, including on-line. This particular product is manufactured in all color temperature variations from full color temperature correction blue (CTB) to full color correction temperature orange (CTO). CTB and CTO both start from the lightest shade of color ranging from "eighth" color temperature correction to "quarter" color temperature correction to "half" to "three-quarter" and finally "full" color temperature correction. The manufacturers of gel material provide little swatch books including every color they manufacture, for free. Accompanying each gel sample is information regarding wavelength in nanometers, transmission, and for the color correction gels, they include the degrees of mired shift.

The top manufacturers that produce the gel products are Lee, Gamproducts, Inc. and Rosco. Lee has been, for years, the industry standard for most motion picture applications. Gamproducts is also geared to motion picture. Conversely Rosco is commonly used for theater or stage applications. It all comes down to cost and preference.

Color Correcting for Skin Tones

As mentioned, the primary function of color correction is to correct for unnatural color spectrums within an image. This brings us to the skin tone factor. If within the images captured, there is more orange than normal, our beautiful twenty-eight-year-old Monica will appear liver-diseased as she sips her glass of wine. Conversely, if the color spectrum is shifted too far into the blue, Monica will have a grayish-blue hue to her skin and appear oxygen-starved. Neither of these looks would be desirable for our bistro scene. This means our first concern would be to correct the color of light so skin tones appear natural and healthy. If, indeed, the scene is filmed mid-day near interior windows and mixed with practical interior and tungsten-lighting instruments, there's going to be some serious color temperature issues that will affect the overall look of the scene, including skin tones. The mixing of color temperatures is not necessarily a bad thing. It is just a concern when situations or scenes demand naturally colored skin. So what do we correct? The light coming in from the windows or the lighting instruments, or both?

For the no/low budget production, it's very unlikely that we'll be applying ten roles of gel to the bistro's windows. If, however, we did use that technique, it would be accomplished by using roles of full CTO or 85-Sun gel to convert the 5600K daylight coming in from the windows to match the interior tungsten lighting instruments of 3200K. This approach would be more expensive than most no/low budget productions would care to pay. That being said, we'd no doubt be inclined to go the easier, cheaper route. That would be to gel and/or correct the color temperature of all the tungsten lighting instruments inside, which would be accomplished by using full CTB (full-blue) to balance the interior light to the daylight coming in from the windows. Then by using a 5600K daylight balance setting on the camera we would have a matched color balance between the interior tungsten light and the predominating 5600K exterior light influence.

There is one other factor to deal with, the bistro's built-in practical lights. These lights are referred to as "house lights." We have a couple of choices, either shut them off or leave them on and correct for the color they emit as well. If we leave them on we may need to take the time to re-lamp the house lights with daylight-balanced bulbs or gel them. But again, this would all depend on what was given and what it would look like when finished. For this scenario I'd be inclined to leave the house lights off and add our own. In this case, we would have the production department bring additional practical interior source lamps designed for photography and have them strategically placed.

Full blue gel over a tungsten 3200K lighting instrument may correct the light to 5600K daylight, but it's not going to work well for skin tones. Full-blue is too blue when trying to capture natural looking skin. Achieving natural skin tones in this case will probably require a couple of steps. First up, rather than using full-blue on our tungsten lamps designated for our key lights, we'd want to use half-blue on the tungsten lights for our actors' faces. The color temperature would then fall into an approximate 4500K scale, creating a more warm hue that would be natural looking.

There is another approach to consider for this scenario and that is to use daylight-balanced instruments indoors. If the production can afford to do so, rent a few HMI instruments. This approach is an easy technique to balancing the interior lighting to the huge amount of daylight coming in from the windows; however, there is still the skin tone issue that must be dealt with. Just like with the half-blue technique we'd use on tungsten lights for more natural skin tones, the same would have to be done with any daylight-balanced HMI type lighting. Instead of half-blue, just the opposite color correction would have to be used. We would want to use half-orange (half-O) for our daylight balanced lights, which would warm the HMIs 5600K daylight to 4500K, again achieving more natural looking skin tones.

The final ingredient for natural skin tone will take place during the color timing process during the postproduction phase of the project. A good color timer will provide the final touches. It is he or she who will add or subtract any adverse color hues, fine-tuning the color of skin without skewing any of the other lighting effects desired.

Note: The before mentioned scenarios are for example purposes only. Actual applications may vary depending on given lighting situations.

The Color of Light, Psychology Speaking

Having a good understanding of color temperature and how the color of light can motivate the audience is what lighting is all about. The color of light is often used to psychologically motivate the audience. For example, let's go outside with our camera and shoot a scene using color temperature to motivate the psychological.

To start, we'll choose a cool, brisk, late winter afternoon for our scenario. There are no leaves on the trees and the sky is grey with high overcast clouds. And let's not have any snow on the ground. The neighborhood will be older, maybe older homes from the1920s, 30s or 40s. That being said, we'll be able to establish a 1950s era scene fairly easy.

We've cleared the street and driveways of all cars except for our hero car. Everything that does not look 50s era or earlier is cleared from our set. The street has been closed to through traffic five blocks deep from the camera's point of view. There are no people. Our hero car is parked in the middle of street halfway down the block. It is a two-tone pale pink and white, 1955 Oldsmobile Delta 88. The driver's door is wide open, the headlights are on and the engine is running. The end of the tail pipe streams white smoke and steam into the cold afternoon air. The camera is positioned down at the end of the street, cranes down from the barren tree branches, stemming from the hundred-year-old oak trees that line the street. Once the camera reaches its number two position, about head height, a slow Steadicam dolly shot begins towards our hero car that sits mid block. As the camera approaches the car, it begins a slow circle around the car, exposing the empty interior as seen through the open driver's door. The camera continues around the car and tracks up the walkway of the adjacent house, revealing the wide open door. As the camera approaches the open door, the old black and white Philco TV plays "Felix the Cat" cartoons. The sound of a teakettle is whistling in the background. The interior of the house is also void of people. End of scene. Save for the fact the 30-second scene has just cost us mega bucks to shoot, we've painted a pretty decent picture of apocalyptic desolation...almost.

Desiring to paint the scene as even more uninviting, we're going to go one step further. Instead of using the typical outdoor setting of 5600K for our color temperature, we're going to use a color temperature setting of 3200K tungsten. The 3200K color temperature setting for the camera will shift the overall hue of the image into the blue spectrum. This blue hue will help sell to the viewer the fact that this is, indeed, a cold lifeless neighborhood. For good measure, during the postproduction process, we'll also de-saturate the colors some. Desolation and despair have now been magnified through color temperature manipulation. Shifting color temperature settings is an easy way to psychologically influence and motivate the audience.

The Color of Light Tells the Story

Designing a color pallet for a film is crucial to the visual aspects of telling a story. While color correction for lighting is at the top of the list of importance, there are also non-color correction colors to consider. Non-color correction materials come in the same thin plastic gel material as color correction gel. These bright colorful gels are often referred to as party gels. Party gels, which are mostly associated with band and stage theatrical performances, can also be used with motion picture lighting instruments in certain situations. These particular colors are used for aesthetics, creating a more distinctive look for a particular setting, such as the red glow of the interior of a tavern, for example; however, these so called party gels may have even more subtle applications. I will now lead you to the 1990 movie release "The Hunt for Red October." Based on the novel written by Tom Clancy and rewritten as a screenplay, this is a classic example of how the color of light is used to help tell the story. Directed by John McTiernan with Cinematographer, Jan De Bont, and Production Designer, Terrence Marsh, together they came up with an ingenious concept for identifying each of the three individual submarines. Since all nuclear submarines pretty much look alike on the showroom floor, identifying each of the submarines for the audience would have been next to impossible. To eliminate such confusion, each sub was assigned its own interior color signature. Red October's interior was lit using blue lighting while the Dallas was given a red lighting scheme and the SSN Konovalov, green. As the scenes cut from one sub to the next, the audience was easily taken aboard each submarine without question as to which submarine they were viewing.

A particular scene we filmed during the "Under the Walnut Tree" production had our lead actress laying in her assigned bed in a small room at a women's halfway house. The room had two beds with a background character sitting up in her bed, leaning against the wall and talking on the phone. For this particular scene, I thought it would help accentuate her uncomfortable surroundings by using odd colored lighting in the room, i.e., reds, deep blues and greens, etc. For this, skin tone was not an issue, in fact just the opposite. The weirder looking the skin tones, the better. The odd colors chosen for the lighting design helped sell our actress's uncomfortable surroundings. Again, the use of unnatural colored lighting can work great for enhancing and motivating emotions. If, indeed, color temperatures and/or party-colored lighting is used for a scene, make sure that information goes on the camera report.

The Camera Report

For all film projects, a camera report must be filled out for each and every roll of film that is sent to processing. Reports are made on industry-standard camera report forms. These forms give the film lab instruction as to how the film is to be processed. They'll require such information as the date, the magazine number, the location, ISO, scene, shot, take, lens, f-stop, filter, footage count and any additional notes. It's the "notes" which are the big thing. If there is something out of the ordinary, those who do the processing and/or color timing, need to know about it. If it was necessary to push the exposure a stop, they need to know that. If the color has been shifted for whatever reasons, they need to know that as well. This same information is just as important when shooting on a digital format.

I had a chance to view a scene from the "Under the Walnut Tree" production after the color timer dude had done his magic. Unfortunately, in the short segment I viewed, the color tone didn't come close to looking anything like what we had shot. The AC failed to make note of the fact that there was an intentional shift in color temperature for that particular scene. The color timer corrected out the morning sunlight we had worked so hard to achieve. Due to the perceived time of day in the scene, it was necessary to shift the color temperature towards a more warm orange hue. The warm shift would help sell to the audience the appearance of early morning. This shift also affected skin tones, making the faces appear more orange. Trying to bring back natural skin tones, the color timer shifted the color temperature of the entire scene back to a more natural appearance. In other words, the corrected shift no longer sold to the audience the early morning time of day.

When capturing scenes using a digital format, a camera report must be made per every download of the memory card, just like with film. Whoever is doing the processing/color timing in the digital world also needs to know what to do, just like with the film lab.

Memory cards should never be able to hold more than thirty minutes of memory. Having a huge memory card that sports eight gigs of memory is a disaster in the making. Memory cards fail. That's just a fact of technological life. Losing up to thirty minutes of footage is bad enough. Losing eight hours is production suicide. That being said, this would suggest having on-hand more than just one memory card. In fact, having no less than five, thirty-minute memory cards should be the ultimate goal. All cards must be numbered or labeled, each marked with a Sharpie from one to five or however many are available. Check the cards often to ensure the card numbers have not worn off. Last but not least, each memory card should be downloaded and switched out every time the camera changes position, even if the card is only partially full.

The D.I.T. (Digital Imaging Technologist) dude or dudette is the person who transfers the information from the card to the computer's hard drive. The process is simple. They receive from the AC, the full or semi-full card and the camera report, in order to begin the download process. He or she hands to the AC at the same time, an empty card in return. The memory cards go from camera to D.I.T. to computer and then back to camera. Note: if there is a snafu with one of the memory cards, it's promptly realized. Be sure to mark any bad cards that are defective, so they aren't accidentally reused. Do not dispose of bad cards as they usually come with a replacement guarantee.

Hire a good D.I.T. There are stories upon stories of "Digital Imaging Technologists" who, for memory space sake, delete takes they think would never be used. Big mistake. The D.I.T. person does not have the authority to delete or edit anything whether on the card or the hard drive. What goes on the card goes on the hard-drive and stays on the hard drive. Never should the Digital Imaging Tech delete, copy-over, or mislabel any files. If more hard drive space is required, then purchase more hard-drive space.

At the end of the day there should be a stack of camera reports a mile deep. Each of the reports are appropriately marked with CARD NUMBER, shot, scene, take, lens, date, etc, and any other notes pertaining to said card. The more information, the better. Hire a good AC who knows the camera report procedure.

A final note before moving on...Even though we've been discussing lighting and its relevance to camera reports and the saving of information, this is as good a place as any to mention...

The same documentation and or sound report for each set-up must accompany each sound card as well. Just like with camera memory cards, sound card information is also transferred to the hard drive and properly designated.

Calibration Tech

Camera and monitor calibrations are absolutely essential to achieving correct color representations. Calibration programs for monitors and in-camera bars are certainly a good place to start. However, another valuable tool known as ColorChecker, manufactured by X-rite GretagMacbeth, also referred to as the Macbeth chart, should be an important part of the DP/AC arsenal as well. X-Rite provides a product that is top-of-the-line and I recommend its use with every lighting and re-lighting set-up. To correctly explain how the Macbeth Chart works, the following excerpt is taken verbatim from the back of the ColorChecker chart. Note: I am not, nor have ever been, a representative of the X-rite GretagMacbeth Corporation.

Using the X-Rite ColorChecker Chart

The ultimate goal of any process of photography, electronic publishing, printing, or television is to reproduce all colors perfectly. However, color rendition is a very subjective matter. Different renditions may be preferred for, different applications and different people may have varied color preferences.

To help meaningful judgments about color rendition, a totally non-subjective standard of comparison is needed. That is why X-rite GretagMacbeth ColorChecker was developed. It provides the needed standard with which to compare, measure and analyze differences in color reproduction in various processes.

The ColorChecker is a checkerboard array of 24 scientifically prepared colored squares in a wide range of colors. Many of these squares represent natural objects of special interest, such as human skin, foliage, and blue sky. These squares are not only the same color as their counterparts, but also reflect light the same way in all parts of the visible spectrum. Because of this unique feature, the squares will match the colors of natural objects under any illumination and with any color reproduction process.

The ColorChecker chart provides an easy way to recognize and evaluate the many factors that can affect color reproduction. To evaluate the effect of varying any given factor, simply compare the chart's color image as it appears on the photograph, television screen, computer monitor, or printed sample with the actual ColorChecker. This comparison may be made visually or through optical density measurements.

Whenever there has been a change in the lighting design and/or color of light, the Macbeth Chart should be recorded just before slating the scene. Bring the ColorChecker up into the frame and have the camera operator roll a few seconds of the chart so the color-timer will have a matched lighting reference to work with. Taking the calibration method one step further, by taping the Macbeth Chart to a true white card for white balance calibration, which includes a focus target, an eighteen-percent grey scale card, and a black trap, is a great way to accomplish many calibrations at one time. There are plenty of on-line calibration tutorials, forums and target examples that explain, in greater detail, this process. This too is a bit subjective as one may have his or her own calibration preferences. The key is to have a consistent reference for all monitors for processing, color timing and/or any creative post engineering effects that may need to be interjected.

At the back of the book, I've included a Kelvin color temperature reference chart. The chart correlates the source of light with an associated Kelvin temperature value.

The color of light originates from God. Making a mess of it originates from man.

Chapter Eleven

LIGHTING IS EVERYTHING

For those of us who aspire to work in a visual arts industry, it is important to understand, lighting must transcend exposure for creativity sake. Light is by its very existence the one true element of creative expression that motivates emotion. For the digital indie cameras of today, lighting is indeed everything.

Assuming you are aware of the basics of lighting, in other words, you have a working understanding of key lights, fill lights and hair lights, you're off to a great start. These photographic basics are just that, basics, a foundation to build from. Even though these basics are based on portrait style still photography, they're also the building blocks for subject lighting in motion picture. By design, three-point lighting is designed to create that ever-important third dimension to an otherwise two-dimensional medium. However, no rules are set in stone; personal preference and creative expression will always trump any textbook rules when it comes to lighting design. In other words, pretty much anything goes. Example: Is there always a need for hair light? No. If the subject doesn't have hair, why light something that isn't there? Remove both hair light and fill light, using only a key light and, viola, yet another artistic expression. Even though the art of lighting is subjective, the basic fundamental rules for shaping and sculpting subjects with light will always be the same.

I get the question from time to time, what makes someone a lighting professional? Is there a college degree for such a position? As a matter of fact, yes. There are a multitude of degrees that can be earned. For example, architectural lighting designers are, in actuality, lighting engineers. They must consider all aspects of light. Whether it's lighting for a mall parking lot so people don't trip and fall on their way to the car, or architecturally designing the lighting for a state-of-the-art bridge, the science of light is as expansive as the universe itself. For those individuals, substantial schooling, and yes, a degree or two, is required. However, for those who find themselves in the visual arts world, the degree earned will be that of audience approval. Now to answer the question, what makes someone a lighting professional. In our world, if you understand exposure and have the ability to creatively paint with light and, most importantly, get thumbs up from colleagues and audiences alike, a lighting dude or dudette you are.

Pizza or Fillet Mignon

Many years ago when I first began working with motion picture lighting instruments, I was visiting one of the grip and lighting houses in town. I had asked the question to one of the rental/sales dudes, how many lights does it take to film a movie? In retrospect, that was a stupid question. That was like asking, how many nuts and bolts does it take to build a car?

Lighting any film is an arduous task, and they all come with their own inherent challenges. Obviously the larger the lighting package, the greater the possibilities, but also the greater the responsibilities. There is also the issue of having a working knowledge of the different kinds of lighting instruments, and of course having to provide power for all of the lights. Believe it or not, the smaller lighting packages that the no/low projects sport, are many times a much greater challenge. If there are only a few lights to work with, it will no doubt require one to come up with even more ingenious ways of making the lights that are available, work much more creatively.

Gaining visual creative insight from the writer/director during pre-production is the first step towards determining what's going to be the best overall lighting package for a project. My argument has always been, if we don't get a lighting package that will do the production justice, why are we even here? Even though the UPM's main claim to fame is to save money wherever possible, the grip lighting package is one of those areas that shouldn't be scrimped on too much. The tight wallet mindset is, many times, the same mindset that counters the goal of actually making money. The old saying, "It takes money to make money," is never truer than in this business. Obviously a truck full of lights isn't going to do much good if there's no money for actors, locations, props, wardrobe or food; however, this is when compromise can sometimes solve the issue of lack.

For us no/low budget indie folks, fifty bucks can be the difference between making a movie and a music video. I'll gladly trade fillet mignon for cold pizza if I can get the lights I need to do the job right.

It's Not the Size of the Package

It is a foregone conclusion that a Lowel lighting kit does not a lighting package make, at least for movie making. Yet, a forty-foot semi, packed to the ceiling with lights is probably out of the question as well; however, having at least a basic grip and lighting package should be in everyone's best interest.

For the "Under the Walnut Tree" production, it was immediately apparent that lighting was not at the top of the list of must-haves. The miniscule package we had to work with was made up of two 1K Fresnels, three 650 watt Fresnels, a 300 watt Fresnel, a 575 HMI, a 1200 PAR HMI and a couple of nook lights. For the grip department we had seven C-stands, eight light stands, a Mombo Combo stand, three bags of grip hardware, a couple of small silks, a 4x4 open frame, a couple of bounce cards and a few electrical supplies. Obviously a few other amenities such as stingers, sand bags, gels, diffusion and clothespins came along for the ride as well.

The package we had to work with would have been too small for a wedding, let alone a movie production. However, there's an old saying, "It's not the size of the package, it's how well you use it." Nothing could be truer, especially in this case. The trick to making what we had work was that we kept most of the scenes fairly small, and when it came to lighting background elements, we used off-the-shelf lighting instruments. More on that coming up shortly.

Unfortunately, the majority of the scenes took place under the huge walnut tree. Filming under the canopy of a 100-year-old walnut tree, with a 1200 PAR HMI, was no easy task. Understand that a 1200 PAR HMI can put out some serious light, but in daylight conditions, it's nothing more than a mouse fart compared to the sun. Our schedule had us shooting both day and night scenes under the monstrous tree, during the months of August, September and October. Because the sun travels across the sky at a rate of 15 degrees per hour, that little 1200 PAR HMI didn't do much, unless it was no more than 8 feet from the talent.

Earlier, I brought up the old saying among photographers and cinematographers that says, "Only fools and beginners shoot at high noon." You may remember that the reason for this saying is that when the sun is directly overhead, faces are as ugly as a mud fence, because of ugly shadows created by the high-in-the-sky sun. So does the high noon rule suggest that filming early in the morning or late in the afternoon are the only options? Yup. That is, unless there are a few scheduled shooting tricks implemented, a few choice lighting instruments, and a few choice lighting control devices are along for the ride.

The only diffusion we had available was a 4x4 full stop and quarter stop silk and one open frame. What we needed was a couple of 40x40 silks to cover the tree, a condor crane and an 18K HMI to replace the sun. The masters were filmed early in the day and all of the close-ups and reversals were filmed at high noon. This put our lead character under a tiny 4x4 silk. To recreate the dappled look of sunlight through the leaves, we used the 1200 PAR HMI gelled with half CTO to key the actor. By aiming the light through a cut branch of leaves, mounted to a C-Stand, we were able to somewhat mimic the dappled sunlight from earlier that day.

The fact that we only had small lights and limited gripage to work with meant we couldn't easily control the lighting for any wide establishing shots. Everyone loves the dappled look of sunlight breaking through the leaves of a large tree. The way the sunlight paints the surroundings and subjects with highlights and shadows is indeed spectacular, except when shooting a movie. Remember continuity? Master shots had to be quickly filmed, early in the day to establish the dappled light created by the leaves of the trees. There was no time to screw around. Again, the director required lots of coverage, even for the establishing wide shots, and normally this would not have been an issue; however, every time the camera changed position, the dappled patterns of light changed as well. So what would have been the alternative? Shoot out of sequence so the lighting was consistent, or shoot in sequence so there was continuity for our lead actress's wardrobe and make-up look. Here's Linda, our lead character, wearing a white mini dress, chained to a walnut tree and living in dirt for, what would be in movie time, a couple of weeks. In continuity terms, she needs to be seen getting progressively dirtier and dirtier throughout the life of the story. Shooting out of sequence would have meant a constant barrage of wardrobe and make-up changes in order to maintain her dirty progression. Nightmare doesn't begin to explain how complex things could have been, especially given the fact we really didn't have a qualified script supervisor. Is it the lighting continuity issues we worry about or the wardrobe and make-up continuity issues we worry about? Choose your poison.

Lighting and the Art Department

It's an obvious fact most no/low budget productions are often going to fall short when it comes to having a decent lighting package to work with. That is why planning scenes along with the production designer can many times help stretch what lighting package there is on hand, a little further.

Soon after being hired for a national commercial some years back, pre-production commenced immediately. Within hours, twenty-five small lampshades were delivered to my shop and the construction of small table lamps began. To creatively light a nighttime sidewalk café scene was the objective. The bustling café was the backdrop for our hero couple, as they walked along the sidewalk. Designed as a dolly shot, they walked facing the lens as the camera dollied with them. Not only was it necessary to light the exterior of the café, sporting its sidewalk tables, but it was also necessary to light the interior because of the café's French style windows that spanned the entire length of the restaurant. There were eight lengths of dolly track, allowing for an approximate 50-to-60-foot dolly track shot. The dolly track had been positioned just off the curb along where cars would have been parked. The camera was angled three-quarters to the rear, which easily framed the couple, the sidewalk tables, and the interior of the establishment. There were eight to ten tables on the sidewalk and the remaining tables were carefully placed just inside the building behind the windows. The building had been vacant and obviously rented by the production company for a couple of weeks. The establishment behind the French style windows was not then, nor ever had been, a real working café. In fact, it was an automotive radiator repair shop just a month prior. Located in the industrial part of town, the production design team went to great lengths in creating the appearance of a French café. That particular location was absolutely perfect in every aspect as the commercial was filmed at night over two nights, on a single weekend. There was plenty of room to work. There was no traffic or nosy onlookers to deal with.

Each of the tables were covered with white tablecloths that had holes punched into the center. This allowed for the zip cord (lamp cord), which was connected to each of the table lamps, to be discretely connected to their power supply. The table lamps each had photoflood bulbs. The rating of each photoflood was 250 watts and tungsten balanced. With other carefully placed lighting instruments both outside and inside, not only was the café ambience sold to the audience as real, the necessary exposure for filming was easily achieved as well. Adding fifty or so extras, who were sitting at the tables eating and drinking, along with dapper-dressed wait staff, the scene easily appeared as though it were any one of New York City's famous sidewalk cafés.

Having the art department included in the café's lighting design helped with the overall lighting process. Obviously, for a commercial of this caliber, there was more to work with. Even still, all projects have a budget they must adhere to. Practical lighting instruments such as table lamps and ceiling fixtures can be used for more than just aesthetics. They can be used for exposure as well.

Shape the Scene with Light... Any Light

If all we did was use broad, paintbrush strokes of light to illuminate our scenes, they'd be illuminated alright, but no more interesting than the lighting at the DMV. Even some of the higher end grocery stores are catching on to the power of designer type lighting. Consider the Gucci-type grocery stores with produce departments that are lit as though they're being photographed for a national ad campaign. They've learned that the better the cucumbers and radishes are lit, the better they sell, especially if they're the kind of grocery store that has to offer low interest financing at the check-out. Since there's so much effort put into the lighting design for a pile of potatoes at a grocery store, doesn't it stand to reason, we should demand the same attention for our works of art as well?

Revisiting the art department for a moment, the practical lights they bring to the program are not only great for exposure value, they can help shape the background, thereby, adding depth to the scene. Lights such as table lamps, shop lights, fluorescent fixtures or other types of off-the-shelf lighting instruments can be used when lighting dark areas in the background.

I received an email from a gentleman from Argentina some years back in which he had asked me if I thought using 300 watt quartz shop lights would suffice for a photo session he had coming up. Good Lord, no, I responded, not unless you like monster lighting. He explained he was not using the halogen shop lights for any of the keys, but only to create pools of light for the background. In that case, yes, I responded, whatever it takes.

An interior/exterior scene that we shot at night just inside the open bay of an old auto shop some years back, demanded everything we had lighting-wise, and then some. There were a few buildings in the background and not much in the way of streetlights or any other lights, for that matter. Not having the budget to rent a condor crane or 12K HMIs to act as moonlight meant we had to be a bit more creative with our lighting design. After the first tech scout, which took place at night, we went back to the location a second time during the daylight hours, and visited with the occupants of the few homes and businesses that would play a part in our background. One house in particular, was approximately a hundred yards or so from where our scene was to take place. In the backyard was a huge old oak tree. The occupants allowed us to place a couple of 1K Par 64s in their backyard, pointed up into the tree. We used medium beam floods in both fixtures and plugged them both into a couple of separate circuits in their garage. The Par 64s lit the tree branches all the way to the top from under the tree. Also we were allowed to place a 300 watt shop light in their front room to light the interior as seen through the front facing window. The shop light was plugged into their outdoor Edison receptacle and fed via stinger (extension cord) through a partially opened window so we could power it up or down, as needed, without bothering the nice people during the night of filming. For another home we replaced their porch light with a 250 watt photoflood, which we simply unscrewed when we were finished. The other background buildings were pretty much done the same way, adding small fixtures either inside or out as needed. All of this was done to help add depth to the scene for the wide master shots. Most people are pretty open to sharing a little power and their property when asked nicely. A ten-dollar McDonalds gift card can go a long way.

For the close-ups that revealed the background, the depth of field was obviously much shallower. For those scenes, we placed 150-watt standard household bulbs, mounted atop C-stands at varying distances and heights in the background, (20 to 50 feet from the lens). By varying each of the lights in placement and intensity, using dimmers, the stand-alone light bulbs easily matched the background lighting seen in the wide shots. The close-ups revealed the background lighting as small, softly lit orbs. Very cool looking.

The point I'm making is that none of the lights used in the background came from our motion picture lighting instrument inventory. The good stuff was used for the foreground and actors.

Personally, I generally like to light or pre-rig the background first and then work my way up to the action; however, if I'm working with a new-to-industry DP, I work just the opposite. To spend countless hours prepping and lighting a background that's not going to be in the shot is a big waste of everybody's time and energy. It always seems to be the young, inexperienced DP who at the last minute changes his or her mind on camera angles.

Having a small lighting package such as the one available for the "Under the Walnut Tree" production doesn't necessarily suggest all is going to be in the dark. It just means we must be more creative when it comes to what instruments will be chosen and how deep into the background we can paint the scene. Creative lighting and adding depth to the background are all efforts designed to bring greater production value. Shaping the scene with light adds visual interest and motivates the audience. It's the extra-added seasoning that makes the difference.

What the Mind Sees

If light motivates emotion, doesn't it stand to reason darkness would do the same? So how does one sell, on film, the illusion of darkness? Walk into any abandoned warehouse that has no windows and after the door shuts behind you, it's blacker than the ace of spades. This is all well and good as long as the camera stays in the truck; hence, the cinematic paradox. Dark may be the desired look, but dark also suggests no exposure value.

Some years back, I was asked to substitute for a gaffer who had taken ill. A scene had been choreographed as a POV (Point of View) shot that began in the kitchen and then traveled downstairs into the dark basement. Thriller films all have these kinds of suspenseful tracking shots, as well they should; it's those kinds of shots that are designed to put the audience on the edge of their seats, so to speak. During the camera rehearsal, the basement lights (house lights) were left on for the walk-through. It was during that time the director fine-tuned the choreography of the camera's travel through the quagmire of basement junk. She made it very clear she wanted the basement dark for the filming of the scene. After the rehearsal, the room was finally turned over to us in grip and lighting. Since it was daytime when the scene was scheduled to be filmed, there was daylight coming in through the small windows at the top of the surrounding basement walls. Certainly agreeing with her that the basement should be dark, I asked how she'd like light coming into the scene to contrast the darkness. She quickly responded with, "No light. I don't want any light. I want it as black as possible down here." With sarcasm, I politely suggested we just roll a few minutes of footage with the lens cap on. We'd achieve the same pitch-black look, thereby, avoiding tripping over all the crap in the basement. Even though not amused by my sarcastic humor, she got the picture. I asked her for some time to perform a few lighting tricks, and that she'd be pleased with the outcome when all was said and done. She begrudgingly agreed and allowed me do my thing.

The crew placed three1200 Par HMIs just outside three of the six upper basement windows, one aiming into the basement from one side of the house and two aiming in from the other side. The remaining windows were blacked out using cut pieces of duvetyn. For the windows that sported the HMIs, we blacked them out as well using Blackwrap. Blackwrap is tin foil, only much heavier duty, and as the name implies, black. Blackwrap is an expendable product that is commonly used to control or flag off unwanted light. Using a screwdriver, we poked a few holes in each of the Blackwrap window coverings. When the HMIs were turned on, the holes in the Blackwrap allowed for shards of light to pierce through the darkness at various angles. To augment the effect, a smoke machine was incorporated to haze the atmosphere. The haze in the air enhanced the beams of light a hundred fold. The narrow beams of light were like sharp white lasers knifing through the darkness. The moral of the story is this: the dark, blacked-out room she so desired had been achieved by actually *adding* light. What the camera captured was the extreme contrast between light and dark. What the mind saw was a pitch-black room.

Extending the Clock… Night Interiors

Have you ever wished there were more hours in a day? It never fails, when a little more daylight is needed, the sun sets. And, unless you're on a sound stage, and unless some big lights are available, there's not much that can be done. If, however, it's more night time that's needed, as long as there's an interior scene or two to shoot, extending night time hours will be much easier, not to mention a lot cheaper.

Night interiors can be extended by using the blackout method. Duvetyn is an opaque black fabric material that is sold by grip supply companies by the yard. Its primary use is to control or block out unwanted light. Cut down to size, duvetyn is a perfect material for blacking out windows. The blacking out of windows is an approach that is commonly used for extending the nighttime hours for interior night scenes. This simple task can be the solution for catching up an already tight schedule.

That being said, there are a couple things that must be considered when blacking out windows. First, if there is a window within camera's view for too long a period of time, unless covered by heavy drapes, it will look blacked out to the audience. Since there are no lights beyond the window to help sell depth, the blacked out window or windows will actually look blacked out. Again, it takes lights to sell the dark of nighttime. When the camera pans across a window quickly that has been blacked out, the illusion of night is easily sold to the audience. To be on the safe side, try to arrange any interior set-ups and camera angles to expose only those surroundings where windows are not visible to the viewer, until it is indeed dark outside. Also, using interior practical lights such as table lamps etc. within the shots will help sell the nighttime appearance.

After dark, the duvetyn can be stripped from all windows. With strategically placed lighting instruments outside the windows, across the street for instance, there can be further depth added to the scene as filmed from inside. Note: You'll want to plan all entrances and exits to take place after dark as well.

Secondly, make sure the duvetyn or any other blackout material is secured properly, completely masking off any unwanted daylight. Do not use gaffer's tape. Gaffer's tape has a super strong adhesive that can remove paint from walls and/or moldings when removed. If taping to painted surfaces is a must, use "paper-tape" only. The adhesion component for paper-tape is a lot less strong and shouldn't remove paint, 98% of the time.

During the filming of a bar scene a few years ago, we were required to build a huge blackout tent surrounding the outside of the entryway. As usual, the only time we could get into the bar to film was on a

Sunday afternoon, during the time the establishment was closed. All but one scene was filmed inside the bar. The scene that got our lead character into the bar, as seen from the exterior point of view, was filmed at another location during actual nighttime hours. It took less than an hour for us to build a ten-foot by ten-foot wooden framework structure around the exterior of the doorway. After the framework was erected, duvetyn was draped over and taped into place. All daylight was carefully masked off, as any light leakage thereof would have obviously spoiled the illusion of nighttime. With the scenes edited together, our lead character drove up and exited his cruiser at night. He walked around the corner and entered the bar. We then cut to the interior of the bar and we saw his entrance from the interior POV. And then, of course, the remainder of the bar scenes took place and then he exited the establishment. To see the whole scene cut together, no one would have ever known we shot the majority of it on a bright and sunny Sunday afternoon.

As mentioned a few chapters back, seasons, locations and global positioning, in regards to the sun, will determine how workable a shooting schedule will be. It can be difficult to extend the daylight hours without some pretty big lights and/or the use of a sound stage, depending on the scenario; however, there is one inexpensive approach that can be used to effectively extend the daylight hour in certain situations. In fact, this is an instrument that doesn't require one ounce of electricity. Allow me to introduce you to the "shiny-board." This one piece of equipment can be a Godsend, provided there is, indeed, sunlight. Where one shiny-board is good, two is better and four is even better.

If the bistro scene were shot as a sunny day instead of a rainy day, shiny-boards and other bounce-light products would, no doubt, have been the lighting instruments of choice, at least for the no/low budget production approach. For example…

Monica exits her building; she stands on the sidewalk waiting for James to exit the cab. As she stands there in all her beauty, we would, no doubt, want the early morning sunlight to backlight her.

The sunlight rimming her long auburn hair will look marvelous, trust me. Using a shiny-board that is positioned in front of her will be her fill light. In other words, we'll bounce the sunlight that comes from behind her back into her face. Obviously, reflecting direct sunlight back into Monica's face would be way too bright and be cause for Monica's blindness. This would not set well with her, her family or her agent. So, instead of bouncing direct sunlight into Monica's eyes, we would want to aim the reflected light into a heavy sheet of diffusion material that separates Monica from the reflected sunlight. The material could be a 4x4 foot sheet of full-white diffusion (216) or 4x4 full-stop silk, or a combination of both, depending on the desired effect. By placing the diffusion between Monica and the shiny-board, the light will be less bright, and more importantly, much softer. Or there is another product that takes another approach to reflecting sunlight.

Grifolyn resembles a tarp, as it is made of a soft foldable plastic material. Less reflective than silver-leaf foil mounted to a 4x4 square board, Grifolyn provides a much softer, evenly reflected light. Grifolyn comes larger than a 4x4 shiny-board, such as 8x8 or a 12x12 foot square sheet, which helps provide a more natural reflective quality. In Monica and James's case, the idea is to light them so they look good. This may also suggest using more than just one bounce light instrument to accomplish the task. The one concern with using bounce light devices is to always be aware of the sun's track. As the sun appears to travel across the sky, so will reflected light change its position. It will take constant adjustment of reflectors and bounce light materials to maintain the desired look.

Reality or Creative Expression

I watched a movie a few months back and during a gathering with friends, I was asked what I thought of the epic drama. Set in 18th century England, I had concerns with the lighting. As the lead character traversed from room to room in her massive castle, I couldn't help but wonder where her key light, fill light and hair light were all coming from. No matter what room she was in, she was always marvelously lit. I found this to be not only unrealistic, but also distracting and annoying. While some DPs light their scenes as though every camera set-up is a wedding portrait, some take a more subtle natural approach. In our real life activities, are we always perfectly lit, with key lights, fills and hair lights? Evidently some filmmakers think we are, whereas, others go for a "less is more" natural looking kind of look. Keep in mind how a production designs and paints with light is certainly up to the DP and the powers that be. Lighting too is very subjective, but does it look believable? That's the question.

Not all DPs mix reality with suspended disbelief very well. In other words, does the lighting design make sense? When my daughter was four or five years old, she painted, with watercolors, a small picture that had purple trees along a hillside covered in orange grass. When questioning her choice of colors, she adamantly persisted that it was her painting to do with as she pleased, and she was right, to a point. It was hers to paint how she wanted, but would it be received well by others? For an outside audience, I'm sure their first thought would have been, "Trees aren't purple, and grass isn't orange." No one, not even me, knew the story in her head. Maybe she was depicting a scene from another planet. If she had titled the painting "Another Planet" I'm sure everyone would have accepted her artistic interpretation of this altered worldview. The same holds true when lighting scenes for a movie. Know the story and know the audience, then paint with light accordingly. Painting a scene with a bunch of weird-colored lights may look cool, (when stoned) but for an audience that's straight, they will no doubt be confused by the pot-induced lighting scheme.

I was watching a made-for-TV movie the other night, and there was a scene depicting a mother and her teenage daughter tied to an overhead pipe in the family's basement. Obviously this was due to a home invasion. In the corner of the basement, directly behind the two ladies, stood a water heater tank. Behind the water heater tank, a bright yellow light glowed. What could possibly create such a bright yellow glow from behind a water heater? Did the water heater have some kind of electrical problem? I've been in hundreds of houses that have water heaters and not one was ever equipped with a yellow backlight. There was absolutely no architectural or motivational reasoning for the yellow water heater light. The bright yellow light was simply distracting. For most viewers it, no doubt, became the focal point for the whole scene. I'm sure everyone watching was waiting for something relevant to come from behind the water heater, but nothing. The weird lighting design ruined the scene.

Is there a relevant or artistic reason to the motivation, the placement and the color of light? Is there, in fact, a purpose behind a particular light, or are we using lights just to empty the truck? Obviously the artistic painting of light can be reason for lights being placed behind water heaters, but one must question. Does placing lights in weird off-the-wall places with bright off-the-wall colors, paint the scene with a kind of Walt Disney-ish flare, and if so, is that the intention? If that is indeed the desired look, then by all means go for it, just be consistent. However, I believe in some cases it may be the actions of an over-zealous, new-to-the-big-leagues DP, much like a kid in a candy store with a crisp ten-dollar bill. For the DP who has worked on nothing but no-low budget indie films with their miniscule lighting packages, and then to be suddenly thrust into a big budget production, the response would be utter elation. With all of the new cool lighting instruments to play with, and all the many choices of colored gels, I guess it's easy to see how one could go nuts and place lights behind water heaters.

Lighting instruments are tools of the trade that we cannot do without. Not only do they maximize the day's shooting schedule, lighting instruments help match shots to shots and scenes to scenes, and last but not least, lighting is the paint we use to journey the audience through space, place and time. Plainly put. Light drives emotion. It is the tool of the trade that we use to feed the big monster that lives in each of us, "creative expression."

Pre-Rigging Saves Time

Take fourteen and we still have to get the reversals. The day is rapidly going away and there's still a company move scheduled. Monica's office scene still needs to be shot. With at least an hour of work to wrap out of the bistro and yet another hour to get across town to set-up for Monica's office scene, it stands to reason, some of the crew needs to go on ahead early and begin the task of pre-rigging the next location.

Having the time, the bodies and extra equipment to allow for pre-lighting is a luxury very seldom afforded to those of us who work in the no/low budget film world. However, when those opportunities do arrive, it can be the difference between a fifteen-hour day and an eighteen-hour day. Depending on how many crew members are available, splitting the team up so that a couple of crew people can get started on the next set-up can certainly help move things along. This, again, is where having a rock-solid location and tech scout performed during pre-production will save the day.

The camera has been moved in for Monica and James's close-ups, and these are the last two set-ups at the bistro. It's very likely the lighting package has been scaled down, which will allow for some of the unused equipment to be on its way to the next location. Having a secondary rigging gaffer is, no doubt, a luxury the no/low budget bunch usually can't afford; however, there will many times be a diamond in the rough that the gaffer can trust to go on ahead. In our case, that diamond in the rough could be an intern who has proven that he or she can walk and chew gum at the same time. Along with a PA or two, he or she can at least move equipment and begin pre-rigging the next location. The remaining crew can easily handle the task of wrapping out of the bistro. Taking lights down, wrapping up cords, folding up and packing away stands can be performed by less experienced individuals. As soon as the director calls wrap on the bistro, the gaffer can be on the way to the next location to do the electrical and help finesse the lights into place.

Filming a night diner scene for a small production required the pre-rigging of lighting instruments due to the diner's limited hours of operation. The additional practical lighting was necessary for achieving overall exposure for the master establishing shots. Over each of the booths and tables, the original lighting fixtures had to be replaced with lighting fixtures in which we could control the brightness. The instruments we used were eighteen-inch china balls, each equipped with 250-watt photoflood standard base bulbs. The lamp cords that powered the lights were hooked to the ceiling directly above each of the tables via drop ceiling hangers. The lamp cords were then strung back across the top of the ceiling, back behind where the camera would be located. Connected to three separate 1K dimmers, the intensity of the lights could then be controlled. Between the coffee counter and the cook's station, we added lighting instruments to help light the wait staff. Four-foot tungsten balanced Kino-Flo tubes were placed end to end under the counter where glasses and silverware were stored. By disassembling a 4X4 Kino-Flo fixture, it was easy to string the tubes individually along the entire underside of the counter out of camera view. Performing these lighting tasks during the diner's normal hours of operation was obviously out of the question. We pre-rigged the diner a day earlier during a time when the diner was closed. When we arrived for principal photography we weren't stalled by having to rig the diner with all of the specialty lights required.

Pre-rigging obviously saves precious time; however, if security is an issue, then such a task may be out of the question. There is also the issue of safety. If using house power, which is the obvious choice for us no/low budget bunch, leaving cables and stingers plugged in and strung from here to there for days on end, isn't going to work either.

A production I was hired to "Best Boy Electric" for had secured an old high school theater to film in. This was for all intents and purposes a somewhat larger project than the average bleakly funded, indie projects of the norm. The school had been closed for years due to asbestos issues, and was scheduled for demolition soon after we were finished. The electrical power requirements for the production inside the theater were quite a bit more than the usual. To create a ring of fire (electrical distribution) around the entire theater required two 900 amp Crawford generators each sporting five-hundred-foot, 4 OT five wire (three phase) banded runs up to the third floor of the building. Each was connected to individual spider boxes. One was placed on the stage floor level and the other was placed on the top seating level of the theater. From there, 600 amp distribution boxes, lunch boxes, dimmers and a 48 channel lighting-board complete with dimmer packs and four dozen "Multi-Pins" were pre-rigged into the overhead truss over the stage. This was a pre-rigging chore that had to be accomplished long before the production moved into the location. There was, attached to the project, a rigging gaffer and a principal photography gaffer, two Best Boy Electrics and a pre-rig team responsible for both installation and removal when the location wrapped.

The point here being, pre-rigging is for some productions a necessity, while others, a luxury. The meticulous pre-production process of the high school theater deemed it necessary to pre-rig for the power distribution. There simply would not have been enough time to perform such a task during the principal photography schedule. This same attention to detail should not be any different for the no/low budget bunch. Identifying those situations where pre-rigging a location is a possible answer to certain scheduling constraints, is obviously worth considering.

The Basic Lighting Package

For the no/low budget film industry, there are some basic grip and lighting items that should always show up to the party. These are the must-have tools of the trade that will always be required. I would even go so far as to suggest purchasing some items. Unless the idea is to produce only one independent film before entering the priesthood, my guess is there will soon be another film following. Considering the cost of grip and lighting rentals and the exorbitant cost of insurance required for said rentals, purchasing some of those have-to-have items can make financial sense. That being said, you may want to consider purchasing some of the equipment used, as that decision will not only save thousands of dollars, but possibly make some money as well. Consider the fact a1200 PAR HMI can cost upward of eight- thousand dollars new, whereas, a used HMI can be purchased for around the twenty-five-hundred-dollar mark. The same holds true for Fresnel lighting instruments, light stands and grip hardware. C-Stands, on the other hand, I suggest should be purchased new. Every used C-stand I have purchased has been nothing but a pain to work with. There is nothing more aggravating than working with an old, worn out C-Stand that collapses under its own weight. For the most part, everything else can be purchased used without too much refurbishing required.

For those of you who are going after investor dollars for your production, purchasing some of the gotta-haves can, many times, be done using "their" money. Grip and lighting equipment can be purchased with the understanding the investor owns the equipment. If the film fails to sell, the equipment can be sold and the investor gets his or her money back. There is also the "multi-film" approach. Say, for example, an investor has a contract that guarantees his or her equipment contribution is based on a three-film return. To rent a 1200 Par HMI for thirty days based on a "one day per week rental" can still cost upward of two hundred and fifty dollars per week. That equates to one thousand dollars in rental for one HMI, for one production, not including the rental insurance. Note: Rental dollars are dollars never again seen, just a thought. For three separate films at thirty days each, that HMI could have been purchased. Investors like collateral and equipment owned is collateral. There are seven ways to Sunday to work deals with investors. The simple fact is, the more ways one can guarantee investment dollars, the more chances the investor's checkbook will come out to play.

It doesn't take a forty-foot grip and lighting truck to accomplish the tasks at hand for the no/low budget indie film project. As mentioned before in regards to the "Under the Walnut Tree" production, if shots are composed fairly tight, a few choice Fresnel heads, a couple of daylight instruments and a few medium duty stands can go a long way. As mentioned earlier in the book, I strongly suggest hiring a DP/Gaffer who's been around the block a few times and truly understands how to get the most out of a small package. For years I ran a small trailer packed to the ceiling with grip and lighting equipment. The package wasn't huge, but contained many of the basic items that were always in need. The package was essentially built out of fruition. After many years of working in the indie circuit, the package became what I felt was the perfect basic package, not too much, not too little. At the back of the book I have listed its inventory by classification for those who wish to emulate.

What to purchase first? This is often the question I get asked when a small independent film company is being established. Going back a ways to the chapter that deals with production value, camera motion equipment such as jibs, cranes, dollies and camera stabilizers are certainly nice to have, but I would strongly suggest purchasing those items that are the most often needed such as lights. Without lights, the production is pretty much doomed before the first "Action." Lighting instruments are difficult to rent without insurance, plain and simple. And insurance isn't always easy to obtain. If there's money that can be used to purchase a basic tungsten/daylight lighting package, you'll be light years ahead. Portable power is another must-have. Investing in a small portable 2K crystal-sync generator will be the one toy that'll be missed most when stolen. Then and only then, a camera crane, camera dolly and process trailer should be considered. These may not be the most glamorous or tech-desired items to own, but without these, that fancy new camera and all of its bells and whistles won't be worth squat.

A man paints with his brains, not with his hands.
Michelangelo

Chapter Twelve

BASIC ELECTRICAL MATTERS

There is no greater frustration than having more lighting instruments than electrical power. Unfortunately, for the no/low budget production, this is more often the case than not. Whether it's renting or purchasing a generator or two, converting 240-volt range/dryer power to 120 volts, or tapping into the household circuit breaker box, it's all done in the name of "more power."

First up is the disclaimer. The writings in this book concerning electrical matters are consistent with U.S. (United States) electrical generating and distribution systems only. If outside the U.S. be sure to check with the country in question pertaining to their electrical generating and distribution specifications, laws and regulations. Also, I am not, nor have I ever been, a licensed electrician; however, I have practiced many electrical duties designated for motion picture. This is due to the fact that the state in which I reside does not require a gaffer or Best Boy Electric to be a licensed electrician. That being said, there are and will always be, situations in any motion picture production where a licensed electrician will be required. Be sure to check with your state concerning the legalities and operational licensing requirements for any person or persons designated to the workings of any on-set film production electrical matters. Notwithstanding, having a basic understanding of how electricity works and how to maximize its availability is something everyone seeking the role of gaffership should know.

The Circuit Breaker Panel is Your Friend

Every home, business or building that has electricity has a circuit breaker box, or at the very least, a fuse box. For whatever reason, no/low budget indie filmmakers have an innate propensity for finding odd, off-the-wall locations to shoot in. That being said, I have but one rule I follow as though it were Gospel. If any building or structure possesses electrical distribution that utilizes old-style asbestos insulated wiring or fuse-type circuit breaker systems, we either find another location or get a generator.

The fact that the larger productions sport large, high amperage generators should indicate there must be good reason for such measures. It takes many large high out-put lights and high out-put generators to operate said lights for large Hollywood type productions. And using a generator is the only way these big lights are going to work. Plugging a 12K HMI into the wall, even if it were possible, would be about as futile as giving a jump rope to a goldfish. Typical household electricity simply doesn't provide enough spark to run lights any more powerful than about 2000 watts, unless of course, one ties into the main distribution box; even then, not enough power to do much on any kind of grand scale without becoming a hazard. One good thing about no/low budget, there's hardly ever the budget for any big powerful lighting instruments. For most small indie projects, if it doesn't plug into the wall, it's not on the truck. This would then suggest someone on the set had better have a clear understanding of how the average household electrical and circuit breaker systems work.

Walking into almost any average bedroom, there are maybe four Edison plug-in receptacles tops, one on each of the four walls.

If asked how many circuits are associated with said room, and the response is four, call the fire department. Counting wall plugs WILL NOT determine how many circuits are associated with any given room. Edison wall plug receptacles are located every few feet for user convenience purposes only. A typical room may have several wall plugs, but only one circuit, maybe two at the very most, depending on the system and the room. The only room, other than the garage, that may have more than two circuits would be the kitchen, and that's a big maybe depending on what year the home was built, and what, if any, electrical improvements have been made. The only way to know how many circuits there are in a particular room is to open up the circuit panel door and visually count how many.

Each of the little black switches inside the door is a circuit. Each are assigned a number and designated to a particular room, as well as their function. Some are designated for built-in room lighting such as ceiling lights, while others are designated for various individual room wall plugs (U.S. type Edison plug-ins). Of course there are other circuits; those designated for heating systems, air conditioning, the range and the electric clothes dryer to name a few.

Once a circuit's designation has been determined, the next big concern is, what is the maximum amperage rating for each circuit? Every circuit breaker has its own specified amperage rating. Each has a numerical value such as 10A, 15A, 20A, 30A and 50A stamped directly on the switch. This numeric value is the maximum amp ratings assigned to that circuit. Exceed the maximum amperage and the switch will automatically shut off, or trip, as it's many times referred to.

To establish how many circuits are associated with a particular room, simply shut off the wall plug circuit designated for said room. Usually posted on a paper label on the door of the circuit breaker panel, are the circuit breakers, listed by number and designated to a particular function and room. If, for instance, the 20-amp breaker that is assigned to the wall plugs in bedroom "A" is shut off, all wall plugs in bedroom "A" should be off; in other words, no electrical power. If, on the other hand, there are still live plug-ins, bedroom "A" has more than one wall plug circuit.

For a larger room such as a living room, there may be two or more circuit breakers designated to the various wall plugs. The designation chart inside the panel door may list the breakers as living room "North Wall", breaker #20 and living room "South Wall", breaker #21, for example. Knowing the amperage rating for a given circuit and knowing what the amperage rating is for a particular light makes it easy to determine the total amperage draw. For example, let's assume in bedroom "C" there is a single designated 15-amp circuit breaker. Here's the question, how many lights can be plugged into bedroom "C"? There is a simple mathematical formula that helps to identify the number of lights, or more importantly, the maximum number of power drawing devices that can be plugged into bedroom "C's" 15-amp circuit.

(100 watts equals one amp of draw.)

While not exact, it does error on the side of safety and the formula is easy and fast to compute. Every lighting instrument has a specific watt rating and is typically referred to by its watt rating abbreviated. Case in point…A 2K light equals 2,000 watts. A1K light equals 1,000 watts. A 650 equals 650 watts. A 300 equals 300 watts and so on. We'll now take the watt rating one step further. Knowing the watt rating of the light and knowing the "one" amp per every 100-watt formula, we can now determine how much draw will be required by a particular circuit in terms of amps. Example: A 2K light equals 20 amps, a 1K light equals 10 amps, a 650 equals 6.5 amps and a 300 equals 3 amps.

If bedroom "C" indeed has a 15-amp breaker, any combination of lights that doesn't exceed the 15 amp maximum rating will work just fine without risk of tripping or shutting down the associated breaker. A 1K lamp and a 300 lamp will equal approximately 13 amps. Two 650s also equal approximately13 amps. Either of the previous examples will be below the maximum 15-amp circuit breaker rating and will not overload the circuit.

As the need for more lights becomes necessary, finding other available circuits also becomes necessary. Having plenty of stingers (extension cords) available is essential for the no/low budget filmmaker's electrical distribution process. As mentioned before, using circuits that come from many other rooms may be necessary to accomplish particular lighting needs. For the basic small to medium lighting package on the typical no/low budget production, ten 50-foot stingers, ten 25-foot stingers, and ten15-foot 12-gauge stingers should be on the truck.

The gauge or thickness of the wire within a stinger must always be a consideration. The stinger must be of a gauge heavy enough to support the load required. For example, if a fifty-foot stinger is required and 20 amps is the needed draw for said stinger, a minimum12-3 wire configuration would be required. The number "12" refers to the gauge of the wires within the stinger and the "3" refers to the number of wires that make up the stinger. One wire is the "Hot" lead (black), and one wire is the "Common" lead (white) and the third wire is the "Ground" lead (green).

Stingers designated for motion picture production are typically rented or purchased from grip and lighting houses. The orange and green extension cords found at the local hardware store are not designed for the abuses typically associated with production type work and should not be used. However, materials necessary to make stingers can be purchased at almost any home improvement big-box store. The industry standard cable is 12-3 SJOOW 300 Volt and can be purchased by the foot. The male and female connectors should be contractor grade and properly attached to the ends of the cable. The wire cable is manufactured with a specific winding and encased with a rubber insulator covering. When the rubber casement is stripped back to expose the three individual 12 gauge wires, the winding of the wire is noticeable. Female and Male connectors are made specifically for this cable winding design. The appropriate connector, whether male or female, should line up easily and naturally with the end of the cable it is being attached to. If the wire has to be twisted and kinked in order to line up with the associated "Hot Common and Ground" connections within the connector, the wrong connector is being attached to the end of the cable. Switch out the connector and it will line up perfectly to the cable.

Multiple lighting instruments sharing the same stinger are commonplace; however, just like with issues concerning circuit breaker overload, the same overload issue must be considered for stingers. Too many instruments plugged into just one stinger can create a fire hazard. Again, as long as the amperage rating for the stinger is not exceeded, there won't be an issue. If more than one light is to be plugged into one stinger, do not use a power strip, always use cube-taps, or three-ways (multi-taps) only. They can be found at most hardware stores for just a few dollars each. Be sure to choose a multi-tap that has a sufficient amperage rating.

Working with a prominent photographer many years back, I had one of my first "what not to do" experiences. The gaffer evidently didn't have any more experience than I did at that time when it came to electricity. Up on the third floor of an old downtown loft, the gaffer somehow managed to draw enough power from each of the small household type extension cords to burn down the entire building. What he was doing was nothing short of entertainingly dangerous. How this guy got so much power from a single source without tripping a breaker is a mystery to this day. Each of the extension cords began melting into the floor like pancake batter to a griddle. Note: Never expect more from a stinger than what it's rated for. Again, for average length and amperage draw demands, use stingers no smaller than 12-3 gauge with 15-amp contractor grade, male and female connectors (Hubbles) at each end. Unless planned, a burning set is never a good thing.

As a multitude of stingers begin their distribution process, the floor of a location can begin to look like a bowl of black spaghetti. Because of the many circuits and their locations, it will be necessary to know at some point, what circuit provides power for what instruments.

Keeping track of what stinger powers what instruments can sometimes be a bit mind-boggling. All stingers and cables should neatly travel alongside the walls from room to room away from any foot traffic. All excess slack from each of the stingers and head-feeders should be coiled neatly under each light stand. There should be one strain relief coil at the wall plug as well. Just in case a circuit does trip (shut off), the neatness approach will make it easier to locate the culprit. Not only does this reduce confusion, this practice is also done in the name of safety. If someone does trip over a stinger, lights won't tip over, power won't become disconnected and/or connectors broken. Note: The head-feeder is the wire or cable that extends from the (head) lighting instrument and terminates at either the male Edison plug-in (120 volt house power) or ballast (HMI).

From Clothes Dryer to HMI

As mentioned before, the "Under the Walnut Tree" production was, for the most part, filmed under a huge one hundred year old walnut tree. The walnut tree is located on a farm out in the middle of nowhere and sprouts from the ground some 250 feet from the nearest power source. Thankfully, the power source was a 240-volt/50-amp shop circuit located in an out-building towards the entrance to the property. The electrical run required 250 feet of large 8 gauge, 4 wire incased cable with grounded male and female 240-volt kitchen range plugs attached to each end. The 240 volts of power was then split into two separate 120-volt, quad-box Edison type receptacles. Each of the two quad-boxes had two 120-volt Edison receptacles wired in, for a total of eight female Edison plug-ins. (One quad-box per 120-volt leg of electrical power.) The two metal quad-boxes were mounted to a board, which kept the electrical junctions off of the sometimes-wet ground. Because the 240-volt shop power was split into two separate legs of120-volts each, any household powered light could be used as long as 25 amps was not exceeded from either quad-box.

Electric ranges and electric dryers can be a great source of power; however, a note of caution: machine shop type 240v sources and/or a kitchen range plug will many times have 50 amp circuit breakers, while most 240 volt electric dryer plug-ins will only have 30 amp circuit breakers. ALWAYS CHECK THE CIRCUIT BREAKER AND AMPERAGE RATING. Also, depending on the state, this particular 240-volt range adapter may be considered illegal. If you're interested in such an adapter, consult a licensed electrician. I'm sure they'd be more than happy to help.

Building Maintenance and the Breaker Panel

Locations such as office buildings, factories, stores, shops and restaurants all have circuit breaker systems, or at least they should. The only difference is their size. Smaller mom and pop type businesses rarely have extremely large electrical power needs while larger building complexes can sport electrical systems that can dwarf the electrical demands of some small towns. This suggests that the tech scout should be performed by someone with a more-than-average amount of electrical knowledge. For the no/low budget filmmaker, it is imperative for a location to have sufficient electrical power. Tech scouts can involve dozens upon dozens of buildings. Take the time to do these correctly and take notes. Relying on memory is cause for many a snafu.

The mom and pop small business, such as restaurants or small buildings, in general, will require a more up close and personal approach to inspecting their electrical systems. In other words, they are the buildings that usually don't have building maintenance personnel. When scouting the location, and if the location indeed meets the photogenic requirements for the production, locate the circuit breaker panel. It will, no doubt, require asking the proprietor as to its location. Once the panel is located, make sure everything checks out. Make sure there are no fuses and no asbestos wiring before giving the location the final thumbs up. Next locate all Edison wall plug receptacles and associate them to their designated breaker switches. What are the amperage ratings for each of the breakers? Are there any 240-volt plug-ins and are they usable? Is the building going to provide the power necessary to operate all lights, monitors, battery chargers etc.? Performing these tasks will determine a building's ultimate fate. If you're the gaffer, don't allow anyone to pressure you into using a location because he or she just has to have the location. If there are questions concerning the safe usage of the building's electrical system, either the production rents a power plant (generator) or they find another building.

For larger buildings, such as multi-story office buildings, there will often be a building maintenance person assigned. This person will be your best friend, as he or she, no doubt, has a finger on the pulse of the building's internal workings. During the location scout, get the building maintenance person's name and number. If the location does meet all photogenic criteria, a tech scout will surely follow soon after. When scheduling the tech scout, call the building maintenance person and schedule them to be present as well. Besides breaker panel location and circuit assignments, it is the building maintenance person who can inform the crew as to any building nuances that may be of concern to the production. Don't forget, maintenance people have lives too. Never assume they're going to be on duty on the day or days of the shoot. Always ask for names and numbers of any others who may be contacted in case of an emergency. Be sure the electrical room is left unlocked and available if filming during off regular business hours. If a circuit breaker does trip, you'll want to make sure it can be easily turned back on, after the problem has been ratified, of course.

Some buildings have printed directly on the Edison wall plug-in bezel plate, an associated circuit breaker designation number, for example, G-103. This is a Godsend as this blatant display of circuitry makes the gaffer's life much easier. Often, other wall plugs will display the same number, making it very clear the other matching numbered wall plugs share the same circuit. These wall-plate markings also make it easy to find non-associated circuits when more power is needed.

Although somewhat expensive, there are "circuit locators" available and sold at most home improvement stores. These are tools that help in associating circuit breakers to their plug-in counterparts.

The Tie-in Kit

For situations requiring bigger demands, such as the use of large output lighting instruments, there is something called the "Tie-in kit." A LICENSED ELECTRICIAN WILL BE REQUIRED. The electrical circuit breaker panel cover can be removed and inside the circuit breaker box is the main power supply that comes in from the power pole or main service junction. A Tie-in kit consists of heavy-duty wire cables (four cables for single phase, five cables for three phase) that come in lengths 5 to 10 feet long. A licensed electrician will attach said cables directly to the power supply, which is inside the circuit breaker box. The opposite ends of the cables that extend from the circuit panel are each equipped with twist-lock connectors that are color-coded. The red and black cable connectors are the hot legs of the power, while the white is the common and the green is the ground. For three phase situations there is also a third leg, colored blue. Again, your electrician will know what to do in these situations. Grip and lighting rental houses provide portable electrical distribution boxes. They are referred to in the industry as distro-boxes. The tie-in's banded cables exit the breaker panel and directly connect, via twist-lock connectors to the power input side of the distro-box. From the distro-box, the power can then be distributed by the use of "Bates Cables" to lighting instruments or other types of power distribution devices. Bates refers to the type of connectors at the ends of the cable. Because there are many makes and models of distro-boxes, the layout of receptacles may vary from box to box. One end of the box may consist of all "Bates" junctions ranging from 30-amp to 60-amp to 100-amp. Also there may be, on one side of the box, 100 amp 240-volt "Bates" type receivers, and last but not least, a typical 120 volt 20-amp household Edison plug-in or two. Distro-boxes range in load capacity; the smaller load capacities can be as low as 300 amps. The larger distro-boxes can sport a 600-amperage capacity. Just because the distro-box may be rated for 600 amps, does not suggest in any way that's the amperage available at the box. It depends on the rated service entering the box. All building electrical service ratings vary. The amperage rating for a particular building could be as low 50 amps. Check with your electrician as to what the allowable amperage draw is for the area and building you're working in.

The "Flow-Through" box, "Duplex box" or "Lunch box" are one in the same. Their nomenclature is dependent on who one is conversing with; nevertheless, they are rated at 100 amps (provided that is, indeed, the amperage entering said box). For our example we'll refer to it as the "Lunch Box." The "Lunch Box" consists of five separate 20-amp, duplex Edison plugs, just like what the household vacuum cleaner plugs into. As mentioned, they are sometimes referred to as "Flow-Through" boxes. This is because they allow power to continue on to or flow through to another box via an additional 100-amp "Bates" cable. For situations that require the power to terminate at a particular location, there is the "Gang Box". In other words, there is no electrical flow-through capability. The 60-amp or100-amp service entering the "Gang Box" terminates at said box. Just like with the "Lunch Box", the "Gang Box" is designed to provide household type 120-volt power via duplex Edison plug-ins for less demanding power applications.

This type of "Tie-in" type electrical distribution application should only be considered when working with a qualified gaffer and best boy electric. It is they who will know the ins and outs of all of the electrical distribution requirements. For every situation, there is always a solution. Even if there is no electrical power within five miles, there is always the generator.

The Generator

From the little 2K breadbox-sized generator to the1600 amp trailer-mounted Crawford power plant, electrical power can always be had. I know that for the no/low budget bunch, asking for a generator is like asking for steak and lobster at Burger King. However, it doesn't always have to be the biggest, most powerful generator on the planet to do the job. Keep in mind that just like with the "Tie-in" kit, the larger mega output power plants will require a qualified generator operator, a gaffer, and a best boy electric, not to mention a few strong backs to carry all of the heavy cable. But for the small "put-put" type generators, as long as someone has a little basic knowledge on how to make the most out of very little, anything is possible.

A few issues must first be well thought out if considering the use of a generator. The first being, what type of electrical power output does the generator provide? The average off-the-shelf, contractor-type generator is designed to provide power for such things as power saws, drill motors and drop lights. None of these types of powered tools require a generator that maintains a constant 60 cycles per second. These cycles per second are referred to in terms of "Hertz." Without going too deep into the subject and sciences of electrical engineering, it is important to understand, what comes out of the average household wall-plug maintains a constant 60 Hertz (60 cycles per second).

So, why is this important to us filmmaker dudes and dudettes? If ever we are going to be using any kind of arc-type light such as an HMI, the 60 Hertz cycle had best be right on the money at all times. HMI is an acronym for Hydrargyrum Medium-arc Length Iodide. HMIs are high-electrical power output, electric or magnetic ballast, ignition regulated, metal halide arc lights. They operate using high-voltage electricity so powerful the electricity jumps or arcs across electrodes that are as much as a quarter of an inch apart. This high-energy arc is similar to that of a welder's arc. If the Hertz cycle varies much, these HMI type lighting instruments will flicker when seen on film.

The HMI requires steady, unwavering, continuous 60-Hertz power, which leads us back to the generator. The contractor type generator that can be purchased at the local home improvement center for two hundred bucks and a six-pack does not provide continuous 60-Hertz power. For these types of generators, the Hertz cycle is not electronically controlled, which results in a varying Hertz cycle. Even though sometimes unnoticeable to the naked eye, the 24 fps camera records HMI light that is powered by an inconsistent Hertz cycle, as a flicker or a wavering intensity of light. This is unfortunate since it means the HMI will require a much more expensive type generator. Generators that maintain a continuous Hertz cycle are referred to as "Crystal Sync." They are equipped with electronics that regulate the Hertz cycle to within one or two cycles of 60 cycles per second, thereby eliminating the flicker.

Grip and lighting rental houses know of this nuance and have capitalized well on this little idiosyncrasy. Besides offering the big power plants to the better-funded productions, they also have available for the no/low budget bunch, the small "put-put" type generators. These are the small contractor type generators, except they are crystal sync. But, that's not all…

The next issue we must be concerned with is maximum power output. In other words, how much power is available for a particular given situation? To determine the amount of electrical power that will be needed, add up all of the total wattage of all the instruments and equipment you plan to plug into said generator. If 2000 watts is the total, then a 2000 watt generator would be required, right? No. Here's the rub, all generators have a duty-rating limit that is less than the posted rating. Example: A 2000-watt generator will not sustain, for any length of time, 2000 watts of draw. The average duty rating for most industry standard generators, large or small, is 80% of the maximum rating posted. In other words, a 2000-watt generator can only sustain a continuous draw rating of 1600 watts or 80% of the posted rating. Remember the 15-amp circuit scenario? That's the equivalent to the actual duty rating for a 2000-watt generator. Not much…Now comes the fun part; scaling back the amount of lighting instruments desired so you don't destroy the little feller. There will always be more lighting instruments than electrical power, that's life for us in no/low budget world. Another put-put, maybe?

Last but not least is going to be the noise factor. Not only does the contractor type generator not run HMIs, but they're too noisy for any kind of filmmaking applications as well. That is, unless silent films are coming back. I can guarantee the sound recorder person will have serious issues if he or she is subjected to a generator that sounds like twenty hotrod lawnmowers just outside the door. Generators designed specifically for the film industry take very seriously any noise ramifications. They are baffled, muffled and insulated to the point of rendering them almost noiseless at a distance of fifty feet. However, here we go again, it's the smaller more portable generators, the kind the no/low budget bunch can afford, that are quite a bit louder. They simply don't have good sound deadening characteristics, due to their smaller size. It's these types of generators that require tenting with sound blankets and/or placing around corners, behind buildings and vehicles, far away from the set as possible, all for the sake of eliminating noise. On that note, security becomes yet another issue to deal with.

While filming a small interior scene late at night in a rather seedy part of town, without notice, the scene went dark right in the middle of a take. The best boy electric ran to see if the generator had run out of gas. Returning to the set in a panic, he announced the generator was no longer there. It doesn't take long for small expensive portable generators to disappear into thin air if unattended. Don't rely on chains, locks or razor wire. A large muscle bound PA sitting on top of said equipment with a loaded gun is the only defense.

One last note on the use of generators: manufactured and available to the public, are small crystal sync generators for rent and/or purchase. Your local home improvement rental house will know of such power plants and will be glad to set you up. For no/low budget filmmaking, these small camp-style generators, while not all that powerful, can certainly be better than nothing at all.

Fire Protection or Wet Mess

One thought that deserves serious attention is fire safety. And, I don't mean burning the place to the ground. A very posh hotel nestled in the downtown area was the location for a rather large film production a few years back. As big lights were brought in and placed, it quickly became obvious that no thought had been given to the fire sprinkler system overhead. All motion picture lighting instruments, save for fluorescents and LEDs, get very hot. If hot lights are placed too close to fire sprinkler heads, umbrellas will be the fashion statement on set. In the case of the posh hotel, their million dollar oriental rugs became nothing more than large expensive sponges. Always look up; try to place lighting instruments far away from such fire sprinkler systems. For added assurance, Styrofoam cups can be used as insulators to protect sprinkler heads from excessive heat. By taping (use paper tape only) a Styrofoam coffee cup over the sprinkler head in question, the sprinkler head will be somewhat protected. It is also smart to monitor the ceiling's temperature. By hanging one of those large, round yard thermometers from the ceiling and next to lights and sprinklers, extreme temperatures can be easily detected. The lowest temperature-rated fire protection sprinkler head is 135 degrees Fahrenheit. This is the temperature at which fire protection sprinklers are designed to do their job, sprinkle. Personally, I never allow the ceiling temperature to exceed 110 degrees Fahrenheit. Always assume the lowest temperature-rated system is in place and again, never completely rely on Styrofoam cups to protect a location from such a soggy disaster.

> *There is no substitute for hard work.*
> *Thomas Alva Edison*

Chapter Thirteen

THAT'S A WRAP

Your first movie is probably going to be the most memorable achievement of your career. It will be the first accomplishment that'll mean more to you than graduating Harvard. There will be disappointments and frustrations beyond imagination. With egos the size of small solar systems, who in their right mind could expect anything less than uncontrolled chaos? All of the extreme highs and all of the extreme lows are cause enough to question one's sanity. Yet, one continues to venture deeper and deeper into this weird world of make-believe, as though pulled by some cosmic force. Why did I choose such an endeavor? Why did I succumb to such a calling? I could have been a night clerk at 7-11, but no. There is that all consuming creative angst that just doesn't get satisfied until one is knee deep in production. It's only when principal photography begins, with the echoing shout of "Action" that you will feel as though your destiny is finally at foot.

Today, no/low budget films are spit out like the morning paper, but do they have the "it" factor? Are they truly the stories that are told like none other? The answer is simple, if they're planned to be as such, then there may be a good chance they can be the golden nugget one so desperately seeks. After all, magic does happen from time to time, especially when planned. Everything in this book can be summed up in one word, "preparation." Not properly preparing for such a project can only lead to one thing, disaster. If the story is indeed good and there is indeed a worthwhile product, then, and only then, will rewards be realized. As cool as the "Crew T-shirt" is, in the end, it's only worth the thread and ink with which it's made. But if that's the only badge of honor, the only award, the only tin-soldier left standing…Wear it proudly; you'll have earned it.

Ensuring a Successful Production

Just to recap, here are a few top things to think about when considering the production of your first film. As with all things worthwhile in life, there is a cost associated with filmmaking. Not only does the cost come in the form of dollars and cents, it comes in the form of time, hard work and expertise. The movie making process demands a handful of professionals who know what to do, what to get and how to get it done. If you're about to embark on a movie making adventure, you need people who have the experience and qualifications necessary for a successful outcome. The bottom line is, it's going to take more than cold pizza and red licorice to lure those who are experienced to your side of the fence. It takes money. Professionals in this industry have dedicated their lives to learning their craft and have an aversion to working for free. If you realize, first off, it takes money to secure a place in the world of movie production, you're light-years ahead of the norm. Trying to do it any other way is pure unadulterated fantasy run-a-muck. That being said, the hardest part of filmmaking is raising the funds to accomplish such a task. Either get schooled on the art of raising money or find someone who already knows the tricks of the trade. Without money there is no production, plain and simple.

When the money has been raised, spend it wisely. I cannot begin to tell you how many times I've been witness to first-time producers spending their money as though they're drunken sailors home on leave. Not only are the funds needed to get the production through principal photography, the money has to get through post production as well. As much as possible, spend the money in all the right places. A forty-thousand-dollar car chase scene for a fifty-thousand-dollar movie won't work. The only way to accomplish this is to get with those who know their craft, the "department heads" and UPM, and round-table the crap out of the script.

We discussed early on the ramifications of a bad script. There are no boobs so spectacular as to save a horribly written story. If the storyline sucks, the movie will surely suck as well. If you've written your first epic and you feel a full-blown production is in the not-too-far future, get a second, third and forth opinion, before going any farther. Make sure all who read it are non-biased and will give you honest feedback. If it takes rewriting the thing seven ways to Sunday, so be it. Think of it this way; every story has already been told in some fashion or another. It is up to you, the writer, to find yet another way to tell the same story, only much better. Also, consider the feasibility factor. If you have scenes within your script that incorporate exploding buildings, outer space and chariot races in 4000 BC Rome, you may want to put that script on the back burner for awhile. In other words, keep it real. Don't bite off more than you can chew. There is an old saying based on the acronym K.I.S.S. (Keep It Simple Stupid). Words to live by for your first production.

As far as the movie short goes, if the goal is to submit an entry into the festival circuit and see how it does, okay, I guess. Just don't expect anything in return but a little recognition, if you're lucky. Frankly, I find trying to produce a movie short is like trying to purchase a disposable boat. They're very hard to get financed and they're only fun for a very short time. They are, for all intents and purposes, un-sellable and when all is said done, they soon become a DVD that sits on a distant shelf collecting dust. When is the last time you spent money at a theater to watch a fifteen-minute movie?

If the desire is to produce a feature and sell the finished product for a profit, hire a "B" list actor for a day or two. Having a recognizable personality associated with a product will help guarantee interest, if not a sale. It's a good idea to factor in a ringer role way back when writing the script. Just don't make the character so precise that only Denzel Washington will do. Many "B" list indie film actors have a box office value associated with them. It may not be much, but some is better than none.

For the rest of the actors and actresses in your epic, choose only those who have experience. Promising Uncle Vince a part in your movie, just so you can use his pick-up truck, will turn around and bite you, big time. If Uncle Vince is a must, give him a role a monkey can pull off. In other words, don't give him any lines. Explain to him the biggest part of acting is 95% behavior and only 5% words. That should suffice, and don't wreck his truck.

Rehearse, rehearse and rehearse some more. The actors we all love to see on the big screen make their job look so easy. It's not; trust me. The talent we, in the no/low budget world can afford to hire, will need rehearsal time. Again, unless there is ample time for rehearsal on the set, this is a task that should be performed during pre-production.

Pre-production is the backbone of any movie production. Allow for plenty of time to accomplish all pre-production tasks appropriately. This is the time, if spent well, that will determine the success of the entire production. There is nothing more frustrating than running into snafu after snafu because of a lack of planning. Pay attention to and address the details early on and the production will benefit greatly.

Choose locations that are affordable, workable and accessible. Get permits when needed and "guerrilla" only those scenes that are small and insignificant enough that ditching them in an emergency is no big deal. Be realistic with all aspects of choosing a particular location. In other words, perform location scouts and tech scouts that mean something. Don't settle on a location just because it looks cool. Where there is one location with a certain look, there is most assuredly another. What good is a location that has no electricity, no parking and no bathroom, and sits fifty feet from a noisy airport?

Always record all principal photography footage on a format that has the best resolution possible, if indeed you're going the digital route. TV sets are no longer yesteryear's big-box cathode-ray tube TV's, they're huge flat-screen monitors that take up an entire wall and reveal every detail good or bad. That being said, if what is being captured is captured using crappy equipment, it is crap you'll have magnified, one-hundred-fold.

All motion picture productions will require some kind of a grip and lighting package to draw from. To attempt to film a movie without lights is like trying to fly a plane without wings. Motion picture lighting has been around since the days of Edison for a reason. Lights are not only needed for exposure, but for matching lighting scenarios as the sun darts across the sky, and to paint emotion and mood for the audience.

We have not discussed much about sound, but it too is as important to the successful outcome of a project as the proper operation of the camera. Hire a sound recorder who knows his or her craft well. Not only should he or she know the ins and outs of good sound recording, but they should also come with their own equipment. And that would be professional, industry standard equipment. While on the subject of sound, consider early on, the scoring or music style and music bed your production will require. Remember, unless you're planning on having someone compose original music, much of what is out there is copyright managed. In other words, if you plan on using a Snoop Dogg song, you better check with Snoop Dogg first, otherwise be prepared for a visit from Snoop Dogg and his legal team. Sound effects fall into the same category. You cannot take the gunfire effects from another movie and interject them into your movie. Again, that would be considered a copyright infringement, punishable by death. Maybe not death, but severe nonetheless. There are plenty of sound-sweetening engineers out there, who will be glad to assist, for a fee of course.

Learning the right way to approach this industry will be worth its weight in gold, as you continue to grow in the knowledge and creative options thereof. Don't expect a blockbuster right out of the gate with your first production. Those kinds of flash-in-the-pan wonder flicks are one in a million. And it never fails; it's usually the once-in-a-lifetime, shooting star type movies that present to the producers, years and years, if not a lifetime, of unsuccessful followers. They're always trying to unsuccessfully recreate the illusive magic that fueled the success of their first unwitting winner. Be satisfied and proud of your accomplishments when you do complete your production, even if it doesn't sell for millions. There are many who have gone on before who do not have that accomplishment to boast. When all of the work, necessary involvement and dedication to such an endeavor is truly realized, the majority turn tail and run as though faced with a death sentence. If it were easy, everyone would be making movies, at least those who have real artistic and creative potential.

Under the Walnut Tree, Where to go from Here

When all was said and done on the "Under the Walnut Tree" production, the project did get completed. It started as an experiment to see if a film project can be done without a budget and the answer is… NO. In the end, it did indeed cost. Not only did it cost in terms of money, but also in friendships, time and nerves. After all out-of-pocket expenses and deferred pay agreements had been calculated, the final tally came to over $100,000.00, which is a far cry from "No Budget." For some, that may not even qualify as no/low budget. With a week's worth of pick-up days, and a last minute ringer drop in, the project is complete and ready for distribution. Yes, distribution. As it stands right now, there are more than a couple of distributors interested in the film, who are willing to pay more than just a few dollars for the product… Go figure. Would the writer/director ever take on such an endeavor again? No. With all of the fights, frustration and technical snafus, it's a miracle the project ever made it past day one. It is this, and this alone, that is proof of one thing; there is obviously a deep seeded desire and passion to being a part of such a crazy, goofy industry. Was a project such as this truly worth all of the hassles? We'll see…a half a million dollars heals a lot of wounds.

Monica and James

For Monica and James, they have reconciled their differences and have since moved from the city. They now live just outside of Napa in northern California. Monica gave birth to twins last March, a boy and a girl. Both have dark hair like their mother and are already crawling around like drunken midgets. James and Monica opened their own bistro; however, since the arrival of the twins, James does most of the work. Nonetheless, business is good and life goes happily along…

For the rest of us, "That's a wrap," as they say in Hollyweird.

For some it's the end… For others, the beginning

Grip and Lighting Package

Transportation
> 1 16' fully Enclosed Utility Trailer
> Rear barndoors/curbside access

Camera Motion
1. 1 Matthews doorway dolly
2. 1 Set speed wheels (skateboard troughs)
3. 4 Lengths Dolly Track

Carts
1. 1 Does-all cart
2. 1 Head cart
3. 1 4x4 cart
4. 1 Taco cart
5. 1 Stand cart

Grip Camp
1. 1 10'x10' EZ-Up tent
2. 1 Propane heater
3. 2 Folding tables

Lighting
All Fresnel heads include
barndoors and wire scrims
1. 2 1200 Par HMI's
    Head-feeders, lenses and ballast
2. 2 2K BJ's (8 inch 2000 watts Fresnel)
3. 2 Mighty Moles (2000 watts open face)
4. 3 1K Baby (1000 watts Fresnel)
5. 5 Tweenies (650 watts Fresnel)
6. 3 Betweenies (300 watts Fresnel)
7. 2 1K Nook Lights (1000 watts open face)
8. 4 Par Cans (PAR 64)
9. 1 Ellipsoidal (750 watts/focusable lens)
10. 2 2X4 Fluorescent shop lights (5/8"pin mount)
    daylight and tungsten bulbs
11. 10 18" China Balls
12. 1 Martin High-Output Fogger
13. 1 Flame bar (charlie bar)

Stands
1. 10 C-Stands
2. 2 Junior Low Boys
3. 2 Hollywood Combos (Double Riser)
4. 2 Mombo Combo's (24' reach)
5. 10 Beefy Baby's (w/rocky mountain leg)
6. 5 Kit (Medium Duty (triple riser)

Grip and Hardware
1. 4 Cardellini's (end jaw)
2. 4 Mafer clamps
3. 2 Quacker clamps (platypus)
4. 4 Furniture clamps (w/bar clamp)
5. 2 Branch holders (baby pin)
6. 4 Foam core plates
7. 5 6" Baby plates (nail-ons)
8. 4 3" Baby pins
9. 10 Ceiling hangers (w/baby pin)
10. 2 Poultry brackets (pinocchios)
11. 2 Baby offsets (baby pin)
12. 2 Junior offsets
13. 2 6" Baby extensions
14. 2 12" Baby extensions
15. 2 18" Baby extensions
16. 2 4½" Gobo heads (lollypops)
17. 4 2½" Gobo heads
18. 2 2x4 Wall spreaders
19. 10 Motorcycle tie-down straps
20. 20 #1 Grip clips (spring clamps)
21. 20 #2 Grip clips (spring clamps)
22. 20 #3 Grip clips (Spring clamps)
23. 10 Anchor Pins (bull pricks)
24. 4 Assorted lengths Speed Rail
25. Assorted Speed Rail fittings
26. 20 Tennis balls (Eye Protectors)
27. Assorted Bungee Cords

Reflectors
1. 2 42" Reflectors (soft/hard)
2. 4 12"x12" Mirrors (w/baby plate mounts)

Frames

1. 2 12x12 Frames (w/elephant ears)
2. 2 8x8 Frames (w/elephant ears)
3. 2 4x4 Open Frames (Opal Frost)
3. 2 4X4 Open Frames (250/Half White)
4. 2 4X4 Open Frames (216/Full White)
5. 2 4X4 Open Frames (clean)

Frame Kit Textiles

1. 2 12x12 Frames
   1 Silk (poly)
   1 Solid
   1 Grifolyn
   2 Double scrims
   1 Single scrim
2. 2 8X8 Frames
   1 Silk (poly)
   1 Solid
   1 Grifolyn
   1 Elvis (gold lame)
   1 Pricilla (silver lame)
   1 Lisa Mari (gold/silver checker)
   2 Double scrims
   1 Single scrim
3. 1 4x4 Frame
   1 Full stop silk
   1 Quarter stop silk
   2 Doubles
   1 Single

Flags and Scrims

1. 4 4x4 Floppy flags
2. 2 2x6 Cutter
3. 2 10"x42" Cutter
4. 2 2x3 Flags
   2 2x3 Full stop silks
   2 2x3 Double scrims
   1 2x3 Single scrim
5. 2 18"x 2424" Flags
   2 18"x24" Full stop silks
   2 18"x24" Double scrims

1 18"x24" Single scrim
6. 1 Set Dots and Fingers

Electrical

1. 2 Range Plug Adapters
2. 4 1,000 Watt In-line Dimmers
3. 4 600 Watt In-line Dimmers
4. 20 50' Stingers (Extension Cords)
5. 10 25' Stingers (Extension Cords)
6. 15 Cube Tapes
7. 10 Ground Lifts
8. 5 Pig Noses (light socket adapt)
9. 10 Crossover mats (cable)

Gripage

1. Apple Boxes
   8 Full Apples
   4 Half Apples
   4 Quarter Apples
   4 Pancakes
2. Wedges
   (30 leveling wedges)
3. Blocking
   (30 2x6x8 Blocks)
4. 21 Cup blocks
5. 4 Boards (2x4x8)
6. 6 Milk crates
7. 10 Furniture blankets
8. 10 15 Pound sand bags
9. 10 25 Pound sand bags

Expendables

1. Gel Rolls
   (CTB-Color Temperature Blue)
   1 Roll Full CTB
   1 Roll Half CTB
   1 Roll Quarter CTB
   1 Roll Eighth CTB
   (CTO-Color Temperature Orange)
   1 Roll Full CTO
   1 Roll Half CTO

1 Roll Quarter CTO
1 Roll Eighth CTO
1 5gal. Bucket
   Assorted CC Gel Cut Sheets
(Neutral Density Gel
   1 Roll ND 3
   1 Roll ND 6
   1 Roll ND 9
2. Diffusion Rolls
   1 Roll T1000 Tracing Paper
   1 Roll 216 Full White
   1 Roll 250 Half White

Color Temperature Chart

1700 – 1800K   Match Flame

1850 – 1930K   Candle Flame

2000 – 3000K   Sunrise / Sunset

2500 – 2900K   Household Lamps

3200 – 3500K   Quarts Lamp

3200K – 7500K   Fluorescent

3275K Tungsten Lamp 2K

3380K Tungsten Lamp 5K/10K

5000 – 5400K   Sun: Direct Sun, Noon to 2 p.m.

5500 – 6500K   Daylight - Sun and Sky

6000 – 7500K   Sky: Thin White Overcast

7000 – 8000K   Outdoor Shade Areas

8000 – 10000K   Partly Cloudy to Cloudy

CPSIA information can be obtained at www.ICGtesting.com
Printed in the USA
LVOW010622041211

257727LV00005B/15/P